D1193623

THE PRACTICE OF
CATHOLIC THEOLOGY

THE PRACTICE OF CATHOLIC THEOLOGY

A Modest Proposal

✠

Paul J. Griffiths

*for David
with warm regards
Paul
27 Sep. '16*

 The Catholic University of America Press · Washington, D.C.

Copyright © 2016
The Catholic University of America Press
All rights reserved

The paper used in this publication meets the minimum requirements
of American National Standards for Information Science—Permanence of
Paper for Printed Library Materials, ANSI Z39.48-1984.
∞

Library of Congress Cataloging-in-Publication Data
Names: Griffiths, Paul J., author.
Title: The promise of Catholic theology : a modest proposal /
Paul J. Griffiths.
Description: Washington, D.C. : Catholic University of America Press,
2016. | Includes bibliographical references.
Identifiers: LCCN 2016026416 | ISBN 9780813228907 (pbk. : alk. paper)
Subjects: LCSH: Catholic Church—Doctrines.
Classification: LCC BX1751.3 .G75 2016 | DDC 230/.2—dc23
LC record available at https://lccn.loc.gov/2016026416

this book is an offering
to the church of Jesus Christ, which subsists in the Catholic church
to those who think and write about the LORD in the church's service
to those who think and write about the LORD outside the church
and to the LORD, who has no need of it

omnes cognitiones famulantur theologiae

CONTENTS

ACKNOWLEDGMENTS

I had help with this book from Carole Baker, Brendan Case, Charles Gillespie, David Bentley Hart, Joe Lenow, Bruce Marshall, Chuck Mathewes, Francesca Murphy, Shifa Noor, Lauren Winner, and two anonymous readers for the Catholic University of America Press. I am grateful to these kind and generous people, and I absolve them from complicity in error (all responsibility for that is mine) and implicit assent to positions they don't hold. I am grateful, as well, to the Catholic Theological Society of America, which invited me to give a plenary address to its annual meeting in 2014, from which this book has grown; to my colleagues and students at Duke Divinity School, who provide me a theologically stimulating place in which to work; and to an enthusiastic and helpful group of doctoral students at the University of Virginia in May 2015, who were kind enough to give a late draft a stern and instructive reading.

PREFACE

This book had its origin in a plenary address given before the Catholic Theological Society of America in June 2014. That address's title was: "Theological Disagreement: What It Is and How To Do It." It was published in *Proceedings of the Catholic Theological Society of America* 69 (2014): 23–36, and some few paragraphs in the present book bear a close verbal relation to what was there published; I am grateful for permission to reuse them here. The lively discussion the talk received upon the occasion of its delivery, and subsequently, led me to think that it might be useful to expand it into a short book. The CTSA address dealt with a particular topic: theological disagreement. This book includes that topic in a broader consideration of what theology is and how it should be learned and performed.

This book is not a primer in Catholic theology, or any other kind of theology. There are plenty of those; the world stands in no need of another, and it is in any case beyond my competence to write a good one. Rather, this is a how-to book: if you want to learn how to do Catholic theology—to become a contributor to that beautiful and elevated thought-performance—this book tells you what to do. Do what it says and, other things being equal, you will be a Catholic theologian.

There are not many books like this. It might be that there are none. Guides for aspiring Catholic theologians tend to assume all kinds of things—for example, that only Catholics, or only believers, or only the baptized, or only those with an active sacramental life, or only priests, or only bishops, or only the morally virtuous, or only men, or only women, can, should, or would want to do Catholic theology. Such assumptions—some of them are manifestly false, and all are rebutted, more or less, in the course of this book—add layers of obfuscation and complication to the relatively simple task of explaining what it is you need to know and be able to do in order to do Catholic theology. The only qualifications necessary for doing it, as this book presents the activity, are that you have the knowledge and skills appropriate to the task. That is a liberating vision, or so it seems to me. It also permits a kind of clarity otherwise unavailable.

Catholic theology, as understood here, is an intellectual skill, and is like all other such skills in requiring some know-how and some knowledge-that. Its distinctiveness is given by what it is about, which is the triune LORD of Christian confession. Otherwise, it is not special, and the means of acquiring skill in it are also not special. That is exactly what makes it available to anyone who wants to do it. Catholics should be pleased that this is so.

I write this book as a Latin-Rite Catholic, and for those who aspire to do Catholic theology with the Latin archive and the Latin liturgical books as their principal authorities and interlocutors. There are Catholics (Byzantine Rite, Chaldean Rite, Malabar Rite, Armenian Rite, Coptic Rite, Anglican Rite, and others) for whom some parts of the Latin archive (for example, the Latin liturgical books and Latin canon law) have a different authority than they have for Latin-Rite Catholics. For thelogians belonging to these rites, the archive looks different, if not in every respect then at least in many. I do not comment further on these differences in the body of the book, but it is good to bear them in mind.

THE PRACTICE OF

CATHOLIC THEOLOGY

§00 TERMS OF ART

Every piece of writing uses terms of art. This is a work about theology which is also itself occasionally a work of theology, and so its terms of art are theological.

✦ The church is the institutional sacrament of Jesus Christ's saving work and presence in the devastation, subsistent in the Catholic church and participated in most fully by those in communion with the bishop of Rome.

✦ The devastation is the created order damaged by the double fall, of angels and humans; once it was a beautiful cosmos, now it's a damaged world.

✦ Doctrine is the church's public teaching on matters of faith and morals; it's to be received by the faithful as a gift and used by the unfaithful, extra-ecclesially, as a proper part of the Catholic theological enterprise.

✦ A god is any putative member of the class of gods; the words (god, gods) are always written here with a lowercase "g," unless in a quotation where it's otherwise.

✦ Grammar (Christian-theological) is the lexicon and syntax that inform Christian talk and writing about the LORD. Like any other grammar, it's fuzzily rule-governed.

✦ Interpretation (theological) is the always-provisional act of reading, glossing, and expounding the words in which the church's doctrine is given to the world; and of doing the same to the words of scripture, which, for the believer, are the LORD's words, and for the unbeliever are acknowledged to function as such in the doing of Catholic theology.

→ The LORD is the god of Abraham, Isaac, Jacob, Jesus, and Mary, the only actual member of the class of gods; the word (LORD) is always written here in uppercase to show that it's a name. It does the same work as the Hebrew tetragrammaton. Pronouns are never here substituted for the name unless in quotation or paraphrase of a text that does.

→ Pagans are all and only those who aren't Jews, aren't Christians, and aren't Muslims.

→ Speculation (theological) is the always-provisional act of offering to the church positions and arguments on matters of importance to its life on which there is (as yet) no doctrine.

→ Theology is reasoned discourse about the LORD—*logia* about *theos*, that is, in Greek; or *sermo de deo*, in Latin. What it is and how to do it are the principal topics of this book.

---

§01 THEOLOGY: INTROIT

Theology is reasoned discourse about god (or the gods) aimed at cognitive intimacy with what it's about. Theology's Christian instance is reasoned discourse about the god who is the triune LORD, the god of Israel who became incarnate as Jesus the Christ. Its goal is the same: cognitive intimacy, to the extent possible, with the LORD it's about. This is a stipulative definition, of theology generically and of Christian theology specifically. It's responsive to etymology and usage, but nonetheless, like all definitions, stipulative. Other definitions are possible, some among them, including some held and advocated by Christians, incompatible with this one. This one leads somewhere. Others lead elsewhere. Assessing this one, or any of the others, involves assessing the thoughts it suggests and evaluating the tracks along which it sets thought moving. If metaphor is language's dreamwork, stipulative definition is language's (and therefore thought's) engine and pilot.

---

§02 DISCOURSE

A discourse is a set of words, spoken or written, in some natural language. This paragraph is an example. Discoursing, running around with words (from Latin, *discurrere*), is something most of us—we human creatures—do a lot of. It's one of our most deeply-rooted and widely-practiced skills. It isn't the only way we communicate—there's gesture and music and the visual arts; neither is discoursing only or even most often communicative. Whatever its uses and whatever its place among our other behaviors, discoursing is among our most distinctive skills. It's begun early, performed eagerly and habitually, even compulsively, as soon as learned and until some external obstacle—usually death—prevents it. We groom one another with words; we speak to ourselves if there's no one else around to hear.

Some few among us die without learning the skill; that's always because of damage or accident, and is cause for lament. Some, even fewer, learn the skill and then renounce it, vowing silence and refusing to speak or write, in some cases for the better part of a life. That may be cause for celebration. But for most, the production and exchange of words, of discourse, is an ordinary and essential feature of life, close in its regularity and frequency to breathing. We don't easily imagine life without it, and even relatively short periods of its absence, whether of one's own or that of others, tend toward the actively painful.

Unlike breathing, discoursing is a learned skill. Human infants need almost no training in order to be able to breathe, but without a good deal of it they don't learn to speak or write. They need to keep company with writers and speakers, and thereby to be catechized. Lacking that, they remain dumb; having it, the style and savor of their talk and writing is inevitably and deeply inflected by those of their catechists. The style-signatures of every human creature's speech and writing are marked by those of their teachers and exemplars in those matters, whether they know it or not, and whether they've tried to eradicate those marks or not.

Discourses may be categorized and marked off one from another by form or tone or style or audience. Soliloquizing, for example, is what it is because it's spoken in solitude; it doesn't matter what it's about. Similarly for sonneteering, which follows a precisely-defined poetic form; and for stump speeches, which are distinguished by having a particular audience and purpose; and for the list, which belongs to a peculiar genre; and so on. These discourses aren't individuated by topic. A list can be made of, a sonnet composed about, and a stump speech given about (almost) anything.

But discourses may also be circumscribed, classified, and recognized by what they're about, which is to say by their topic. Geological discourse is what it is because it treats the material composition of the earth; political discourse is made such by being about the *polis*; biological discourse has life, *bios*, as its topic; and so on. Those are categorizations by topic. There are usually things to say about the register, tone, diction, audience, and style of particular instances of any of these topic-defined discourses—it's perfectly possible to write biological sonnets, for example, just as it is to make political lists. But the sonnethood or listhood of such things isn't what makes them biological or political. That's given by what they're about, by their topic.

Sorting discourse into kinds—this is love-talk, that's a poem, you're cursing now, that library is full of law books, he likes to gossip, she's lying, they're talking politics, we like to share a joke, now I'm writing theology—is, just like discoursing itself, a learned skill. It's one that most language-users perform intuitively, without noting that they're doing it or how they're doing it, and certainly without need to make their doing of it explicit. We all code-switch effortlessly enough, addressing our lovers differently than our colleagues, differently again than our children, and differently yet again than someone with whom we're performing a commercial transaction; we write in one way when texting a friend and another when polishing a piece of prose for publication; and we do these things without, usually, having to give them much thought. Similarly, we usually know when a certain topic is in play, and respond appropriately to its presence. Interjecting a discussion of prosody into one about the weather is odd; to do it requires special reasons, or a lack of familiarity with local conventions. Mostly, we don't, couldn't, and have no need to, analyze, label, or describe the kinds of discourse we're producing or responding to. We simply speak or write, in various forms and about various things. Only specialists classify and organize discourse into kinds, and their work has very limited use.

Sometimes we encounter an unfamiliar discourse, one that we're unsure how to perform or respond to. We might be puzzled because of an unknown lexicon. In such cases, the language spoken is comprehensible in the sense that the syntax of its sentences is clear—we can identify conjunctions and nouns and adjectives and adverbs. But what's being said is incomprehensible because we don't know the lexicon: we don't know what's being talked about, even if, judging by tone and gesture and syntax, we have a good idea of how it's being talked about—chattily, excitedly, argumentatively, contemplatively, with ennui, and so on. Perhaps the people we're listening to are talking cricket or baseball or macroeconomics or theology, and we have as little acquaintance with the lexicon proper to those discourses as with the street-plan of a town we haven't been to. Or perhaps we find ourselves called upon for the first time to make verbal love to someone, and find ourselves unsure how to do it, sounding to ourselves, when we try, like someone butchering a half-understood dialect, and this even though we have some passing familiarity with what's supposed to be said in such situations. Or we find ourselves in the presence of those using a highflown diction we've not heard before; we understand, to some degree, what they're saying, but are puzzled as to why anyone would say it like that. We might, in such situations, turn away as soon as we can, in search of more familiar discourse, discourse we're at home in and can participate in without stress.

Another reaction is possible. We might be intrigued. We might find the opacity and difficulty and oddity of what we're hearing a challenge. We might seek elucidation. Any of those responses amounts to asking for catechesis: if we want elucidation, and especially if we want to learn how to talk and write in those ways ourselves, we have to place ourselves under instruction with the thought that this is a skill we'd like to have. That is always, and necessarily, how a new discourse is learned.

This book is itself catechetical. Reading it shows something of what theological discourse is and what you need to do if you want to read, hear, respond to, and produce such discourse yourself. Like all catechetical devices, this is an imperfect one; also like all catechetical devices, its imperfections aren't what matter about it.

§03 THEOLOGY AS DISCOURSE

One way of individuating discourses is by topic, which is to say what they're about—the world, the city, love, war, grammar, beauty, hatred, the ocean, hope, regret, lament. One topic that people can and do discourse about is god and the gods. And so, if we're individuating discourse by topics, we can reasonably say that one kind of discourse is about god and the gods.

Why might we want to say this? Aren't there many ways of individuating discourses? Why not subsume, for instance, discourse about god and the gods into discourse about imaginary objects? Or into poetry? Why treat it as a kind of discourse in its own right? There are many ways of individuating discourses; none of them serves all purposes; all serve some purpose. This one, the isolation and analysis of discourse about god and the gods, serves particularly Catholic purposes—and perhaps broader Christian ones. Whether it's a good idea to treat discourse about god and the gods in this way depends upon the fruitfulness of doing so; and what counts as fruitfulness itself depends in significant part upon criteria internal to Catholicism. There's no neutral ground upon which to stand in these matters. Discussion of how to divide discourse into kinds, or, worse, argument about which kinds of discourse there really are, without discussion of the purposes of making such discriminations, is wheelspinning. The ruts it gouges are deep.

When a discourse is individuated and labeled by topic, it's ordinarily easy enough to tell when a specimen of it is at hand. The principal mark is the presence of the appropriate lexicon. If words such as "state," "nation," "government," "election," and "democracy" are scattered broadside in some specimen of North American discourse, it's likely enough that the discourse is political: the ordinary lexicon is present. The absence of that lexicon indicates, though doesn't guarantee, the absence of political discourse.

This is a rule of thumb. It isn't a set of necessary and sufficient conditions for recognition. It serves for everyday purposes—it ordinarily suffices, that is, to indicate the presence or absence of geological, or political, or biological discourse. It doesn't demarcate with forensic precision the boundaries between one discourse and another, or provide the means to judge with certainty that a specimen of this discourse or that is at hand. These lacks aren't problems. Most of the time, rules of thumb are adequate to their task, and that's true of this one, too. If the lexicon is present, a reasonable working assumption is that the discourse it belongs to also is; and the extent to which the lexicon is absent is, roughly, the degree to which the discourse is absent.

In the case of talk and writing about god (or the gods), the presence (in English discourse) of the term "god" and its cognates and derivatives is one important mark of the presence of such discourse. A treatise with the title *De deo uno* (on the one god), or one labeled *God is Not Great*, have good first-blush credentials to be considered specimens of god-discourse. And if some talk or writing treats the nature and doings of powerful nonhuman agents, then, because the gods are typically understood as of this kind, it too has first-blush title to be considered to belong to the category. Another mark of god-discourse is the presence in it of the names of powerful nonhuman agents recognized locally: Zeus, Wotan, Krishna, Superman, Paul Bunyan, and so on. When their names appear, it's reasonable to say that the discourse in which they're found is a specimen of god-discourse.

Christians produce a good deal of discourse about god and the gods in this broad and generic sense. It's everywhere in the canon of scripture, where the god of the Jews and the Christians (from a Christian point of view, one and the same—this is a non-negotiable item of Christian doctrine) is carefully discriminated from the gods beloved of and worshiped by others, and where much attention is paid to the nature of the Christian god. That god is represented in the third chapter of Exodus as providing a name in response to Moses's request for the name of the one who is commissioning him to lead Israel out of slavery. That god self-designates as "I am who I am" (*ego sum qui sum*), and tells Moses to communicate that name to the people by saying that the "one who is" (*qui est*) has sent him. This opaque self-designation —an encouragement to think that the one so self-designated is above anything so mundane as a personal proper name—is supplemented in the same chapter of Exodus with something like a title—*Dominus*, the LORD—which becomes, in effect, the scriptural proper name of this god; and then a brief account is provided of the things the LORD has done. The name-giving episode ends with the formula, "this is my name forever" (*hoc nomen mihi est in aeternum*), a formula which can be read to embrace not only the self-designation and its gloss, but also the historical story that specifies what this god has done. This god, the one with this name, is in one sense god, a member of the god-species; but in another sense entirely not so, entirely separated from all genus- and species-identifications; so, at least, the naming-episode can be read to suggest, and so it has been read by a large majority of Christians.

Psalm 95, recited by Catholics at the opening of the daily cycle of prayer, is lyrical and representative on this question: "The LORD is a great god, a great king above all gods." The other gods, whatever reality they may have, are not like the LORD; they aren't the ones who simply are; they can't say of themselves *ego sum qui sum*; their reality is of a different order, and this affirmation, or suggestion, pushes thought about the LORD far and fast away from subsumption into a putative god-species. It's not that the LORD is more of a god than other gods; the LORD is above all gods, other than they, a god by courtesy only, and for linguistic convenience.

The LORD, the one who is, is according to the grammar of Christian discourse, triune, and called, when being so considered, Father-Son-Spirit, which is the *trinitas quae Dominus est*, the trinity the LORD is. The Son is identified with Jesus, also called the Christ. This means, among other things, that the presence of the name of Jesus, the name above all names in which alone salvation is to be found, is another indicator, along with "the LORD" understood as something like a name, of the presence of Christian discourse about god and the gods—which is to say, of Christian theology. LORD, Father-Son-Spirit, Jesus-the-Christ—these are the nodes around which Christian god-discourse coils. These are the principal signs of its explicit presence. They are lexical signs, and because of that they are recognizable to anyone who has been catechized in the lexicon.

Christian god-discourse is not the only god-discourse there is. One of the characteristic forms of Christian god-discourse is the active separation of itself from god-discourse practiced by others—pagan god-discourse, let's call it. This shows that saying there are non-Christian god-discourses is itself a claim proper to Christian discourse. The pagans, those innocent of Jesus or of the self-revelation provided by the LORD to Jews (and perhaps to Muslims), so Christians say, can and do discourse about the LORD, even if not by that name or under the triune description. This is also a claim generally endorsed by pagans observing and thinking about the kinds of discourse there are in the world. They're likely to think—it's hard to avoid thinking—that there's a lot of god-discourse in the world, and that what Christians say about the LORD as Father-Son-Spirit is an instance of it. Discourse about god and the gods, individuated from other discourses by topic and recognizable by its distinctive lexicon and syntax, is no more difficult to recognize and produce than biological or legal or political discourse. It's learned just as they are, and deployed just as they are. The difference is given by what it's about: the LORD. But that difference doesn't exempt it from the category of discourse, or make the modes of its recognition, learning, and deployment in any significant way distinct from those of other discourses.

Christians may, and often do, call discourse about god and the gods "theology"; they may, and often do, include their own discourse about the triune LORD under this rubric. These are good and useful classificatory moves to make. When pagans discourse about god and the gods, Christians can, sometimes do, and for most purposes should, think of what they produce as theology; when Jews discourse about YHWH, the LORD whose name cannot be pronounced, Christians should call what they produce the same; similarly, with more reservations but still not many, for Muslim discourse about Allah whose prophet is Muhammad.

This lexical recommendation—call all speech and writing about god and the gods "theology" and include your own under that label—is made only to Christians. I, the one making it, have no standing to prescribe usage to Jews and Muslims and pagans; they have their own lexical and syntactical needs, which are no business of mine, and rarely the business of any Christian. What they call god-discourse is, therefore, up to them. Even among Christians, the prescription is controversial. Narrower understandings of what "theology" ought be taken to mean are commonplace among Christians, and there are Christian proposals about the word's use incompatible in other ways with the one made here. Nevertheless, there are good Christian reasons for preferring this usage to its competitors; most of those reasons are rooted in convictions about the LORD's intelligibility and availability to creatures.

Theology, according to this proposal, is a discourse individuated by topic. It's discourse about the LORD. The word's etymology suggests this. It's rooted in Greek (*logia* about *theos*), where it means "reasoned discourse about god/the gods," much as "anthropology" means "reasoned discourse about the human" (*logia* about *anthropos*). Etymology isn't dispositive in determining meaning. Usage ought be attended to as well, and here too there is strong support for this way of taking the word. Among the ordinary glosses on *theologia* (calqued into Latin from Greek, and not very much at home there) is *sermo de deo*, "talk about god/the gods." This, for Christians, ought to be the ordinary usage of the word. This understanding of theology is clear, nontechnical, easily understandable by analogy to other words of similar form in English, and a useful thing to offer in response to questions about what theology is. It's at home on the rough ground of ordinary usage. Providing it—theology's about god/the gods, you might say—tells inquirers as much as they'd learn if, puzzled by the word "geology," they were told that it's about the earth.

The principal sign of the presence of theological discourse is the appropriate lexicon. But looking for that lexicon won't always permit Christians easily to decide whether a particular specimen of discourse is about the LORD. Consider the sentence, "there is no god but god, and Muhammad is god's prophet." The term "god" appears in it, which suggests that the sentence is theological. But Christians might wonder, not unreasonably, whether the understanding of "god" informing this sentence is distant enough from a Christian understanding of the LORD as to make it dubious whether it's about the LORD at all, and therefore to raise questions about whether it's theological. The same doubt might be raised about sentences like, "Zeus is king of the gods," or "Krishna revealed himself to Arjuna on the battlefield," or "Superman leaps tall buildings at a single bound."

The mere presence of words such as "lord" or "god" or (even) "LORD" doesn't guarantee that the discourse in which they're found is about the LORD, or even that it's about god and the gods. Some such sentences are sufficiently distant from anything a Christian might consider talk about the LORD—"le malheur a été mon dieu" (disaster is my god), Rimbaud wrote—that it's not reasonable to attend to them as if they were contributions to Christian theology or theological in any but the most attenuated sense. But others, like the sentences about Zeus and Krishna and Muhammad, are harder cases, and might reasonably be considered by Christians, or by those trying to decide what can be appropriated into Christian theology or treated as an instance of such, to be about the LORD. That's so even if they turn out to be false, and even if their speakers deny, or might, that they are about the one Christians call the LORD.

The right line to take here is a relaxed one. If the surface lexical signals are that a discourse is theological, then the first assumption a Christian theologian should make is that it is—that it is in some sense about the LORD, and is therefore grist for Christian theology's mill. This assumption says nothing about whether what the sentence says is true or adequate to its topic. And the assumption is defeasible: further consideration may lead to the conclusion that what looks like theological discourse isn't; or that it is, but that what it says is false; or that it is, but that it can't be accommodated into Christian theology, or isn't useful for Christian-theological purposes. But those are not the places to begin. Christian theologians ought not be in the business of restricting, as a matter of principle, the material they have to work with. Why look gift horses in the mouth? Get on them and ride as far as they'll go.

If theology is discourse about god or the gods, whether or not with knowledge and use of "LORD" as the name, then, as is ordinarily the case with discourses, some of it is explicit about its topic, and some implicit. The LORD's triune nature, the LORD's incarnation as Jesus Christ, the LORD's creation of everything other than the LORD, the LORD's establishment of a covenant with Abraham—these are explicitly theological topics. By contrast, discussion of the habits and rules of conduct proper to human creatures, or of the nature of the created order, or of the norms according to which scripture is properly read and interpreted—these are implicitly theological topics. In discoursing about them, the topic of god and the gods may remain largely in the background; what they're explicitly about is one or another aspect of the created order. This is also true of such topics as the proper way to speak about the LORD, or the nature and extent of the church's teaching authority. This isn't to say that such topics aren't theological. They can be treated within theology's ambit, and when they are, discussion of them may become explicitly theological, which is ordinarily to say that the relations of what they're about (human persons, the *polis*, the created order, literature) to the LORD have become an explicit part of treating them. But still, at first blush they aren't about the LORD, and therefore are at best *theologiae ancillae* (theology's handmaidens).

It's not that every specimen of discourse is either theological or not. Some are explicitly and fully theological; others implicitly theological and occasionally explicitly so; and yet others theology-free except in the most distant and formal of ways. There are many kinds of discourse essential for the practice of theology which are not themselves theological; grammar and mathematics serve as examples. If you want to sniff out the presence of theology, whether because you find the bouquet sweet or repellent, you ought bear these qualifications in mind even though they leave untouched the central claim, which is that theology is discourse about god and the gods, with its Christian instance being discourse about the LORD, the triune one who is.

§04 THE LORD AS THEOLOGY'S TOPIC

Theology is about god and the gods. Christian theology, which is a specimen of theology, is about the LORD, the one who is, who brought into being everything other than the LORD, elected Abraham, led Israel out of slavery, chose Mary as Jesus's virginal mother, and became flesh as Jesus the Christ. In what sense can discourse be "about" this one?

The LORD, on the Christian view, is not a particular, not an object or a being in the world, not a thing, not even the biggest, best, and unsurpassable thing. The LORD does not stand at the top of the hierarchy of creatures, and is not a member of any class or category of creatures. The LORD is, rather, *idipsum*, the thing itself, the selfsame, the one whose properties and actions are, exactly, the LORD as the LORD is. This is not true of me or of you or of any creature. We have properties accidental to ourselves (being here, wearing these clothes, looking at that view, eating this food, reading those books), properties that come and go and could have been otherwise and that we can lose and gain without losing or gaining ourselves. The LORD, uniquely, is not like that; what the LORD has and does is what the LORD is. The LORD has no accidents and no potency; the LORD is eternally, atemporally, *idipsum*, one and the same. That's what it means to be the LORD; to be in any other way is to be a creature.

This estranges the LORD from our discourse. That's because our discourse has evolved for and within a world of contingent particulars, each separate from the others and each, at least in theory, specifiable by its differences from the others. When we speak of things-in-the-world, we do it by talking of kinds and their *differentia*; such talk and writing assumes contingency and potentiality.

The particulars we speak of, including ourselves, could have been otherwise than they now are, once were otherwise, and will again be otherwise. We analyze, categorize, relate, and discriminate these things endlessly, asking ourselves, in moments of self-reflective metalinguistic consideration, what we talk of when we talk of love, and answering always by making distinctions: love is this and not that; this, that, and the other thing are not love. Our language signals in its grammar the world with which and in which it works. It's a world of things that can be discriminated, defined, analyzed, and (perhaps, sometimes, asymptotically) comprehended. The LORD does not belong to such a world. We cannot approach comprehension of the LORD; there is no relevant asymptote.

The LORD is not part of—an element in—the world of contingent particulars, and cannot be spoken of as if it were otherwise. To do so is to make the LORD a creature, and thus to perform idolatry, to think—or at least to imply—that the LORD is a creature. That is a constant temptation for Christian discourse about the LORD. Specifying the proper means of avoiding it is itself a theological topic, and one about which Christian theologians have said and written much. Every such specification must hold together at least the following: that attempts to define the LORD by identifying and listing the LORD's properties and actions necessarily fail; that, nonetheless, we human language-users cannot do otherwise than write and speak of the LORD exactly by writing and speaking of what the LORD is and has done; and that language is therefore necessarily placed under an almost unbearable strain when the LORD is its topic. To forget this estranging linguistic strain is to forget the LORD; to think only of it is to enshroud the LORD in silence, and thereby to make Christian theology impossible. The theological task is to remember and to lament linguistic estrangement without being silenced by the memory and the grief.

Christian theology is about the LORD, certainly; the LORD is its topic. But the mode of this aboutness is uniquely strange, and is so in such a way as constantly to call the enterprise into question. There are liturgical analogues to and models for this estrangement, this performance of what cannot be performed. When Christians prepare to approach the LORD in eucharistic worship, they do so haltingly, repeatedly underlining in the words they speak that what they are about to do cannot be done. Even after the bread and wine have been consecrated before the congregation's face and offered to it, and even after the declaration is made that those who can receive the body and blood are happy—blessed—to be able to do so, the congregation declares that it is incapable of receiving what is offered, echoing, in doing so, the scriptural words of the Roman centurion who asks Jesus to heal his servant: *non sum dignus ut intres sub tectum meum, sed tantum dic verbo et sanabitur anima mea* (I'm not worthy that you should enter under my roof, but only say the word and my soul shall be healed). All theological discourse works under this rubric: *non sum dignus ... tantum dic verbo*. Theologians, whether believers or not, lovers of the LORD or not, need to remember this so that theology, rather than something else, is what they do.

The difficulty about aboutness is deep and, finally, beyond solution. It doesn't, however, call into question the view that it's reasonable to say that theological discourse is about the LORD, and that it's possible to determine, with ordinary perspicuity, whether a particular sentence or collection of them is theological. That's because the criterion is a formal one. A sentence is at first blush about the LORD, and therefore theological, if (though not only if) the LORD figures in it as subject or predicate. The sentence "god was in Christ reconciling the world," and the sentence "I pray to the LORD daily," are both about the LORD in this formal sense. This makes them, at first sight, theological sentences, sentences that belong to the discourse that is theology, even if neither those speaking them nor those hearing them could offer an account of how it is possible for sentences to be about the LORD, much less an account of what the LORD who appears in these sentences is like.

§05 CONFESSION AND THEOLOGY DIFFERENTIATED

Christian theological discourse is about the LORD, and the extent to which discourse is explicitly about the LORD is the extent to which it is, and ought be judged, Christian-theological. But most discourse of that kind is confessional. That is, it's the language of love, whether in the form of endearments, of gratitude for gifts received, of pain and anger for apparently unmerited suffering, of desolation at the LORD's apparent absence, of quotidian exchange in which the ordinary events of the day are told, of anguish at one's own failures and sins and stupidities, and so on. The context for most of this love-talk is liturgical. It's in worshiping the LORD communally, as a body, that Christians most often confess the LORD to the LORD's face and before one another's faces. But it can occur outside that context as well, in private prayer or recollection.

My parish church, for instance, has a small chapel in which the blessed sacrament is reserved. I often pray there for a while before Mass, and every now and then I see small pieces of paper laid before the tabernacle on which someone has written a message, usually an entreaty, to the LORD. Sometimes I read them. Usually they're in Spanish, and a representative sample is, "Dear Jesus, please protect me and my family from everyone who wants to hurt us, and help my son to live a good life." This sort of thing—petitionary, intercessory, ejaculatory—belongs to confessional language. It's a gift of verbal love to the LORD, given in the mode of direct address.

Confessional talk meets the criteria for theological discourse in a very clear way. It's replete with the name of the LORD, and often has much to say by way of identifying the LORD's nature and actions, hoped for or acknowledged. In these ways it's profoundly theological, perhaps the most purely and deeply theological talk there is.

But in another way, confession is not best thought of as theology or called theological. That's because its aboutness is the aboutness of call and response; it's about the LORD in something like the same way that the calling of your name by someone drowning in a torrent and imploring your help is about you; or in something like the same way that the use of your name as an endearment by your lover in moments of passion is about you. Those drowning and loving aren't considering your nature and trying to arrive at an understanding of you. No, they want, and want desperately, you to do something, respond, give yourself, reciprocate, caress, reach out your hand to save them. They're not thinking about you; they're wanting something from you or offering something to you; they're urgently eager to enter into a particular relationship with you. The call and response of lovers is similar. When I say to my beloved that her lips are like a scarlet thread, or that her breasts are like ewe lambs, I'm not telling her something about herself, stepping back for a moment and offering her a considered judgment of her charms. No, I'm caressing her with words, and what I hope for is the caress returned.

Theological discourse is more distant from what it's about than is the confessional caress. It has a different stance. Those trying to talk and write theology are not, as they do so, in the LORD's embrace, eagerly exchanging caresses with the LORD; neither are they clinging to the LORD, desperate for succor. Rather, if they're believers, they're looking at the LORD, trying to see the LORD, aiming for whatever clarity they can get about who and what the LORD is. Or, if they're not believers and think that talk and writing about the LORD is fictional, they're trying to develop their skill at writing a kind of non-confessional fiction, a fiction that depicts a character as fully and precisely as possible. These stances require, typically, a step back. If I want to paint my beloved's picture or offer a verbal sketch of her to a third party, I can't easily do those things while I'm in her arms. I have to distance myself from her, and make of her something she isn't while I'm kissing her—that is, something I can think about, talk about, write about, with the degree of dispassion needed for those activities. So also, changing the appropriate particulars, for theologians and the LORD.

Theological discourse does have and aim for a kind of intimacy with the LORD, but it's cognitive intimacy rather than fleshly or affective intimacy. What theologians are after is knowledge of the LORD. They want to come as close to the LORD, intellectually speaking, as our faculties and the LORD's nature permit, and they use, therefore, the devices proper to the intellect in order to move toward this goal. They make distinctions; they enter into argument; they engage opposing views in order to clarify the lineaments of the correct (as they see it) view; they deploy what they know about other topics in order to illuminate this one; and, inevitably and without end, they produce words—talk and writing are their products. Those engaged in confession are as likely to use other devices: they position and move their bodies, they grasp the bodies of others, they groan and shudder, they speak in tongues, they are silent and immovable. All those, and many more, are proper to confession, whether private or corporate. Theologians, by contrast, seek and offer words that tell themselves and others what the LORD is like. These are different enterprises; they yield distinctively different kinds of discourse; they have different purposes.

All Christians are confessors. They seek to receive love from the LORD and to return it as best they can; they want to be in the LORD's arms and to feel the LORD's lips on theirs. A Christian who did not want this would be like a wife who did not want to keep company with her husband or a father who wanted always to keep his children at arm's length. But Christians don't need theology in this way; theology is to confessional intimacy with the LORD roughly as the analysis of marriage given in the *Code of Canon Law* is to the state of being married. Spouses may want to read the *Code* to one another, and they may even find some mutual delight in learning to offer a precise, analytical account of the state they're in. But it would be a mistake damaging to most marriages to take such learning to be any substitute for the intimacies proper to marriage; it would be an even greater mistake, one that probably nobody is tempted to make, to think of studying the *Code* as what marriage is really about. Similarly, studying theology and learning to produce theological discourse are not what the Christian life is about. Few Christians need be theologians, even if some capacity to understand and respond to theological discourse is, for some at some times, an ancillary aid to the work of the Christian life; and even if understanding is a good.

Theological discourse and confessional talk are both about the LORD, but the mode of their aboutness is different. It's often easy to tell the difference: "My God, my God, why have you forsaken me?" is, it's hard to doubt, confessional language; *unde Pater et Filius simul una sapientia quia una essentia, et sigillatim sapientia de sapientia sicut essentia de essentia* (and so, Father and Son are at once one wisdom because one in essence, and each is wisdom of wisdom as also essence of essence), as Augustine writes in *De trinitate* (from §7.2.3), is, it's equally hard to doubt, theological talk. There are many cases in which the division isn't so clear; there are no bright lines here, any more than there are in the case of dividing implicitly from explicitly theological talk. But still, the difference between theological and confessional talk is often recognizable enough. It's the difference between the offering of a caress and the offering of a description. Theologians are in the latter business.

But, isn't the distinction just offered, between theological discourse and confessional talk, too sharply drawn? Doesn't seeking knowledge of the LORD, the capacity to say true things about the LORD and to reject things that can't appropriately be said about the LORD, require some affective intimacy—which is just what confessional talk seeks and offers? And, in the opposite direction, doesn't the confessor's intimacy with the LORD require some knowledge of—cognitive intimacy with—the LORD whose caress is being sought and returned? Well, yes; but not in a way that calls the distinction here made into question. Confessors do and must know something of the LORD they confess, just as lovers do and must know something of the beloveds they kiss. But that knowledge is not what confession thematizes or seeks, and the actions they perform in offering and seeking intimacy aren't those that knowledge-seekers undertake. The theologian's activities are verbal. Knowing how to go on as a theologian is knowing which words to write (or say) next; knowing how to go on as a confessor or lover may (usually does) have little to do with words. The activities characteristic of each mode of approaching the LORD are different, and it's (usually) easy to see the difference. In the reverse direction the distinction is even easier to make and to see. Those who aspire to do theology, to talk and write about the LORD, need not love the LORD; they need not even take what they say and write to be true. They may perform theology, with skill and passion, under the rubric of mention rather than use, as an enterprise that seems to them experimental or fictional. And they may do so with a high degree of skill.

---

§06 DEFLATING THEOLOGY

Distinguishing theology from confession rightly deflates theology. Theologians too often inflate it. One cause for this tendency is the almost inevitable proclivity of practitioners of anything to think what they do important, and to proselytize for it. Scrapbookers and bodybuilders are as likely to do this as theologians; these three activities are alike, however, in being unnecessary for most and impossible for many. Enthusiasm for them and delight in them needn't require overestimating their importance.

Another cause for inflating theology's importance is the entirely accurate judgment that theology's topic—the LORD—is more important than any other. Those who seek cognitive intimacy with the most important thing there is (not, of course, a thing at all; rather, the giver of being who is the condition of the possibility of all beings and, therefore, of all thought), and who work hard to arrive at and express truths about the LORD, are easily tempted to think and say that what they do is more important than anything else because of the importance of what it's about. Even less plausibly, they may think that everyone—or at least every Christian, or every believer, or some such—needs to practice theology as much as they can. But all this is a mistake. What the LORD wants from Christians is that we return, with love, the gifts given us by acknowledging them as gifts. That's what's important. The intimacy proper to the gift-exchange is what the LORD seeks from us. Cognitive intimacy, by contrast, is, in the post-lapsarian devastation prior to the remaking of the world that follows the general resurrection (these are explicitly Christian theological claims), a pasttime for a few. Those few need unusual intellectual capacities and a good deal of time free from the need to make a living. They provide a service to the church, which does need theology to guard against error, to provide for its pedagogy, and to extend its understanding of the deposit of faith given to it.

---

§07 COGNITIVE INTIMACY

Theologians, in practicing theology, seek cognitive intimacy with the LORD. That's the point and purpose of theology. The skill and single-mindedness with which theologians perform their task is closely indexed to the degree of cognitive intimacy with the LORD they attain. If you do anything well (speak English, write sonnets, play baseball, make love, curse), you approach the end (or ends—some have more than one) for which that thing is done. Some practices, perhaps, have only their own performance as end (nothing hinges here on deciding whether that's so), but that's emphatically not true of theology. It's for cognitive intimacy with the LORD, and performing it well gets you that, like it or not, know it or not.

But it doesn't follow that theologians need to know what their performance gets them in order to be able to do it well. This means that they don't need to recognize or assent to the truth that theology is for cognitive intimacy with the LORD when it's propounded to them in order to be good theologians. These are (instances of) ordinary truths about human beings and what we do. We often, perhaps usually, perform without being able to give an account of what we're doing or of what it's for. The skill of offering such accounts is additional and extrinsic to the skill of performing the practice about which such accounts might be given.

This distinction can be deployed, among other things, to support the view that it's possible for the believing theologian and the unbelieving theologian to do equally (though not identically) good theology. They'd offer, if pressed and if capable, different accounts of what they're doing when they talk and write about the LORD. Unbelievers might say they're mentioning rather than using theological talk—here's how the discourse goes, they might say, here's the next distinction to offer and the next argument to make if you want to pursue that line; believers might say, by contrast, that when they get it right they're coming to know something about the LORD they didn't know before, offering the LORD a cognitive caress and receiving one in return. These two accounts of theological talk and writing are not compatible, but their incompatibility doesn't prevent both groups from doing theology in the sense in play here; neither does it prevent them from mutual instruction.

Catholic theology, in the full and proper sense, may, therefore, be done by those who are themselves not Catholic—so Catholics ought to think, even though many of them do not. If Catholic theology is talk and writing about the LORD responsive to a particular archive and a particular tradition, then there's no reason to limit its performance to those who are baptized, or those in full communion with the bishop of Rome, or those who believe in it, or those who love the LORD. All that's necessary for a theological performance to be Catholic is that it be speech and writing explicitly about the LORD done in response to the proper archive, which is to say with the proper interlocutors. On that understanding it's no harder (and no easier) to decide whether some specimen of discourse counts as Catholic theology than to decide whether it's in English.

Cognitive intimacy with the LORD—theology's end—can be construed in many ways, and necessarily differs (from a theological point of view) here in the devastation from what it will be in the resurrection. Here below we know nothing well, and very little—and with that little largely occluded—about the LORD. Cognitive intimacy with the LORD here, then, is largely a matter of pushing back the darkness, and involves little more than excluding a few of the more dramatic errors that can be made in thinking about the LORD, and in that way removing some of the obstacles to cognitive participation in the LORD. In the resurrection it will be different: we'll know the LORD by vision, directly and without obstacle, as fully as is possible for creatures constituted as we are. That's not the kind of cognitive intimacy sought by theology. Theologians seek and find an altogether more modest kind of knowledge of the LORD.

---

§08 CATHOLIC THEOLOGY AND OTHER THEOLOGIES

Theological discourse is about god and the gods. Christian theological discourse is about the LORD, the triune one who took flesh as Jesus the Christ: it's theological discourse about the god of the Christians. This way of thinking about the matter entails that theology comes in kinds. Some of these are non-Christian, constituted, that is, otherwise than by response to the name of Jesus; and the Christian kind, which is responsive to that name, itself comes in kinds—among which, from a Catholic point of view, the Catholic kind is paradigmatic. No sorting, labeling, or depiction of these various kinds of theology is or can be uncontroversial, but a good deal of clarity can be had about what Catholic theology is and what its practice involves by differentiating it from both other Christian, and non-Christian, kinds of theology.

Catholic theology, as Catholics see it, is the most perfect

expression of Christian theology, and since Christian theology, in turn, is, from that same viewpoint, the most fully developed instance of theology in general, it follows at once that it belongs to Catholic theology to say of itself that it is the most perfect (fullest, least incomplete) instance of talk and writing about the LORD. Things seem different to theologians from other communities, Christian and otherwise, no doubt; but this is what it belongs to Catholic theology to say.

Catholic theologians therefore typically think of non-Catholic Christian theological communities as lacking some goods proper to the prosecution of the theological task, some of which are to hand and in mind for Catholic theologians. This doesn't at all require or suggest that non-Catholic Christian theology has nothing to teach Catholic theologians; it's evident that Catholic theology has learned much in that way, and continues to do so. Attentiveness and responsiveness to the theological discourse produced by non-Catholic Christian theologians ought to be, and sometimes is, a hallmark of Catholic theology. One reason for this is that the LORD may have revealed things about the LORD's self to non-Catholic (and non-Christian) communities which remain hidden from Catholics (it's Catholic doctrine to affirm this of Jews). Another is that Catholics may need the help of non-Catholics in coming to a fuller understanding of the revelation with which Catholics have been gifted; Augustine claimed that he learned from the books of the Platonists in these ways, and, arguably, Thomas Aquinas treated Aristotle's corpus in a similar way. There are many other instances.

How, then, does the variety of Christian theological traditions and communities appear from a Catholic point of view? What are its principal kinds, and what are the labels appropriate to them?

The first and most spatially and temporally extended non-Catholic species of Christian theology is Orthodox. Its separation from Catholicism came, formally speaking, during the eleventh century, when the Latin churches and the Greek anathematized one another. There is no single Orthodox church, administratively speaking, even though the various self-governing patriarchates (almost) all recognize the theoretical primacy of the patriarch of Constantinople; and so a full accounting, from a Catholic viewpoint, of Orthodox theology, would attend to the particularities of theological style and archive that distinguish one patriarchate from another. In general, however, though very inadequately, the Orthodox archive is like the Catholic in the authority it gives to the canon of scripture, and to the deliverances of the first seven ecumenical councils. There is no similar magisterial structure, which means that little can be said by way of generalization about that archive, other than that there is one and that it is large. The speculative archive, too, while largely common for the early centuries, diverges markedly after the fourth century. One thread of commonality in a good deal of Orthodox theology is anti-Catholic, and that fact has its effects, varied and complex, on the reception and use of the Orthodox speculative theological archive by Catholic theologians. Nevertheless, Orthodox theology is, from a Catholic viewpoint, responsive to the fullest and richest version of the Christian archive of any non-Catholic kind of Christian theology. Its weight is significant and its potential for instructing Catholic theologians great.

The second significant subkind of Christian theology is Protestant. This is even more internally differentiated than Orthodox theology. The various kinds of Protestant theology have their origin in anti-Catholic reform movements that began in Europe in the fifteenth century. They share, therefore, a deep anti-Catholicism; that's almost a defining characteristic of Protestant theology in a way untrue for Orthodoxy, deep though anti-Catholicism also runs there. The Protestant textual archive, like the Catholic, gives primacy to scripture, but with few exceptions has an attenuated canon in the case of the Old Testament, and, usually, different views about the authority of scriptural versions. If any of the ecumenical councils are accepted as authoritative—and for many Protestants, none are—it is no more than the first seven. Many Protestant communities are self-conscious in their rejection of any magisterial authority: the church is not, for them, a teacher, and is not guided by the Holy Spirit to teach. Those that do preserve some remnant of magisterial authority usually focus it on the teaching office of the bishop; and even that is weakened and attenuated. The Protestant archive of speculative theology is also substantially different from the Catholic. Some Protestants recognize as authoritative in some sense the work of Christian speculative theologians during the first four or five centuries of Christian history; but after that, the archive is largely empty for the millennium separating the Council of Chalcedon (451) from the fifteenth century. And then, the speculative theologians most often consulted, though without any broad agreement as to their authority, are the system-builders of the Reformation, such as Luther, Calvin, and Zwingli.

Apart from Orthodoxy and Protestantism, there are many other non-Catholic but arguably Christian theological communities and traditions. Some (Donatists, Nestorians, Arians, Albigenses) are no longer extant, but of considerable historical importance. Others are lively still (Lefebvrites). But none approach the significance, for Catholic theology, of Orthodoxy and Protestantism.

There are also non-Christian theologies. How do Catholics sort and label those? For Catholic theologians, first among non-Christian theologies is the theology done by those who belong to the people of Israel, those who are inseparably and intimately covenanted to the LORD as the LORD's chosen. This theology is the interlocutor of most importance for Catholics, more, even, than the theology done by non-Catholic Christians. "Jewish theology" is a convenient, though not uncontroversial, shorthand label for it.

This theology is, beyond any Catholic doubt, explicitly responsive to the LORD: it knows the name of the LORD, and this, as well as the LORD's incarnation as a Jew, the composition of almost all the texts of the New Testament by Jews, and the intimacy of the relations between Jews and Christians these past two millennia, sometimes mutually fruitful but too often conflicted and violent—the violence almost always visited by Catholics upon Jews—makes Jewish theology an essential contributor to Catholic theology. Its claims, arguments, tropes, and methods may often provide matter for Catholic disagreement; there's much of that in the tradition. They may also provide occasion for admiration, delight, and instruction; there's some, though not enough, of that in the tradition. In all cases of serious Catholic engagement with Jewish theology, which ought be frequent and deep, the first Catholic response ought to be one of grateful attentiveness.

Catholics ought also recognize theology done by those who embrace the identifier "Muslim" for themselves and the theological discourse they produce, and who typically think of Muhammad as the LORD's prophet, and the Qur'an as the LORD's speech. This, as in the case of Jewish theology, is a Catholic description, which is to say one serving Catholic theological purposes. There's no Catholic doctrinal position on the significance Islamic theology has for Catholic theology, or on what Islam is, and this makes of Islam and its theology a puzzle for Catholic theologians in a way that Judaism and Jewish theology aren't. Catholic theologians cannot say with certainty about their Islamic counterparts that they know the LORD's name; or that Muslims are intimate with the LORD, elected by the LORD; or that Muhammad is a prophet of the LORD. But neither can they affirm the contradictories of these propositions as anything other than speculative positions. These are, for Catholic theologians, open questions, ripe for theological speculation. As with Jewish theology, Catholic theologians ought assume an attitude of humility before the particulars of Islamic theology, and before its theologians, with the thought that there may be in the theology they write and speak something to learn from and admire. This doesn't exclude the possibility that Catholics might identify and argumentatively engage errors or imperfections in this or that Islamic theological position, or in the deep structure of Islamic thought about the LORD.

Theology is also done, Catholics should think, by many who are historically unrelated to Abraham. In the Mediterranean basin, for example, during the human past of which there is any record, there were substantial traditions of thinking about, analyzing, and depicting god and the gods by those who were not Abraham's descendants or kin. There are theological performances by Platonists, Aristotelians, Pythagoreans, Egyptians, Babylonians, Hittites, Cretans, and many others. In what we now call Western, Central, and Eastern Asia, massive bodies of literature about god and the gods were composed in Sanskrit, Tamil, Chinese, Korean, Tibetan, Japanese, and many other languages, from the second millennium B.C. onwards. And from Africa, Australasia, and the Americas, prior to the colonial incursions, there is widespread evidence of thought and talk about god and the gods over a long period of time, even if there is (almost) no literary deposit of that talk. Much of this material is properly theological, even though all of it, by definition, is ignorant of the LORD's name. The ignorance of the name on the part of these many theologians doesn't mean that they fail to write and speak about the LORD when they theologize; Catholic theologians should assume, as a working hypothesis, defeasible when evidence suggests, that these theologians are writing about the LORD, and should also assume that there's something to learn from such theologies. This has certainly been so in the past. Among the principal stimuli for Catholic advances in understanding the LORD's self-revelation have been encounters with and expropriations of traditions of thinking about the LORD developed largely or entirely without connection to Christianity.

What ought Catholic theologians to call theological discourse performed by those historically unrelated to Abraham, and therefore ignorant of the name? They aren't Christian; neither are they Jewish or Islamic. A traditional Christian label for them is "pagan." All theology, according to this usage, that isn't Jewish, Christian, or Islamic, is by definition pagan; from a Christian viewpoint, that fourfold division is comprehensive in the sense that no theology falls outside it. The word "pagan" has some disadvantages. It can seem insulting; and it necessarily embraces a broad range of non-Christian theologies. The commonalities between, for instance, Santideva's theological work in eighth-century India, and the theological understandings evident in the thought and practice of the Australasian indigenous peoples are few, and this means that finer discriminations within the broad category of pagan theology are necessary if Catholic engagements with particular instances of it are to be fruitful.

This Catholic way of classifying theologies yields a fundamental division into Jewish, Christian, Islamic, and pagan theologies, with finer divisions findable and usable as needed within each of these categories. Catholic theologians are doing a kind of Christian theology, and among their tasks is clarity to the extent possible about the sources, methods, and authorities proper to the kind of Christian theology they practice; also among them is clarity about what differentiates Christian theology from other kinds of theology, and, concomitantly, eagerness to learn from those other kinds. The theological work of non-Christians is a gift to the church, and ought always be embraced and treated as such. That is no less true when it turns out to be unacceptable: understanding which gifts cannot be accepted, and why, prompts clarity otherwise unavailable about which can, and why. That's a kind of clarity Catholic theologians ought be eager for, and it can only be had by way of serious engagement with non-Christian theology.

§09 CATHOLIC THEOLOGY'S KINDS

Catholic theologians, more than Protestant or Orthodox ones, like to divide their own theology into kinds according to such variables as purpose, method, audience, and topic. They also, and with less pause than they ought, treat the categories they use to label such divisions as if they were natural kinds, and as if they described enterprises sufficiently distinct and self-enclosed that no theologian should trespass the boundaries. These are mistakes. The Catholic theological enterprise—of thinking, writing, and speaking about the LORD in response to a particular archive and tradition—has a unity that subtends and overcomes any of its divisions, and its thoughtful and energetic practice pushes theological performance through the barriers that separate the proposed subdivisions. The categories used to label Catholic theology's subkinds are heuristic rather than prescriptive; they map the theological territory rather than provide a photographic image of it, and the lines that separate one kind of theology from another are like the lines that separate states and nations one from another. Such borders appear on maps and have political and practical reality, but they are not features of the landscape and their locations and their names vary considerably—sometimes dramatically—with time. Nonetheless, some unenthusiastic mention of the map's current configuration is necessary because the borderlines on it constrain practice and affect training. It's about as easy for Catholics to cross the border between systematic and moral theology without the proper profile and degree as it is for immigrants to cross that between Mexico and the United States without the proper papers, imaginary though the borders are in both cases.

There are kinds of Catholic theology defined (mostly) by method and purpose—by, that is, how they're done and what they're for. There are, at the moment, four widely-used labels for theologies of this kind: fundamental theology, philosophical theology, dogmatic theology, and systematic theology. All these terms of art for kinds of theology have a short history: they're effectively unknown before the seventeenth century, and they became popular as a way of mapping (some of) the theological territory only in the nineteenth. Nevertheless, they are at the moment lively enough, and since their ordinary understanding opposes them to one another, they need to be discussed together.

Fundamental and philosophical theology are alike in prescinding from church dogma, and in attempting to depict, argue for, and elucidate what can be known and said about the LORD without assuming Christian conviction or Christian knowledge. Fundamental theology is concerned with what founds the structure of thought and talk about the LORD—matters such as the LORD's existence, the dependence of the world upon the LORD, and the means by which human creatures can come to know the LORD independently of the church. Philosophical theology is essentially the same; attempts to differentiate these two have, typically, a desperate air. The deep similarity between the two is evident in the fact that they're both understood, definitionally, as not-dogmatic and not-systematic. Those varieties of theology, the systematic and the dogmatic, are explicitly responsive to church doctrine: they presuppose it, state it, elucidate it, propose orderings of it, and so on.

Dogmatic and systematic theologians are like those who write and argue about the particularities of baseball while presupposing the revelatory gift of the baseball rulebook; fundamental and philosophical theologians are like those who attempt to establish the nature of games in general and ballgames in particular, without attending to the givens of any particular game. The two groups need one another; the lines that separate what they do are far from bright.

Fundamental, philosophical, dogmatic, and systematic theology are not defined by topic; they can and do address any theological question permitted by their methods and goals. Other Catholic theological kinds are, by contrast, defined exactly by the topics they address. There's *Christology*, which treats the LORD as incarnate; *pneumatology*, which treats the LORD as Spirit; *trinitarian theology*, which treats the LORD as triune; *ecclesiology*, which attends to the LORD's post-ascension body in the devastation (it has *sacramental theology* as one of its most significant subkinds); and *eschatology* and *protology*, which depict and analyze the LORD's relation to spacetime and the culmination of the LORD's purposes there. All these are directly and explicitly about the LORD, and are therefore theology in the strict and proper sense. They have as *ancillae*, intimate and necessary servants, such theological topics as *mariology*, which deals with the mother of the incarnate LORD. All these, topic-specific as they are, can be undertaken by dogmatic/systematic theologians, or by fundamental/philosophical ones; a Christology, for example, undertaken by a dogmatic theologian would look significantly different from one written by a philosophical theologian, even though both would be about Jesus. And again, all these topics bleed into one another; it's not possible to treat Christology without also treating pneumatology; and separating mariology from trinitarian theology is artificial.

There are also topic-specific kinds of Catholic theology whose focus is upon us, we human creatures, as affected and effected by the LORD. These, too, are properly theological, but their angle of vision and concern is different from those mentioned in the preceding paragraph. They include: *moral theology*, which attends principally to the theological norms that govern human conduct in an attempt to understand how the fact that humans are the LORD's creatures affects what we may and ought do; *ascetical theology*, which treats the norms and disciplines by which humans can deepen their intimacy with the LORD; *hamartiology*, which analyzes human sin and humans as sinners; *soteriology*, whose concern is with the nature of human salvation; and *political theology*, perhaps best taken as a subkind of moral theology concerned with the proper understanding and ordering of the *polis* in light of conviction about the LORD.

And then there are Catholic-theological kinds largely defined by their focus upon one or another of the LORD's modes of presence to the world. Of first importance here are *biblical theology*, whose object of study is the text of scripture as revelatory of the LORD and the LORD's purposes; and *historical theology*, which treats the LORD's presence in history, most often in the texts that belong to the Christian archive (other than scripture) and the events that constitute the life of the church extended over time. Each of these has overlaps with all the other kinds; and none of the other kinds can properly be undertaken without in part doing so as a biblical and historical theologian.

These labels for subkinds of Catholic theology are in common use in the guilds that govern and order professional theological work among Catholics. Aspirants and neophytes perforce locate themselves and their work within one or another of those kinds. But the labels have no other significance, and good theological work trespasses the boundaries as a matter of course.

§10 DOGMATIC AND SPECULATIVE THEOLOGY

There is one way of dividing and ordering the theological enterprise with more than heuristic or pragmatic significance for aspiring and practicing theologians. That is the distinction between dogmatic and speculative theology. The former has the task and purpose of understanding and elucidating what the church teaches of relevance to some particular question—or, as an ideal but unrealizable goal, what the church teaches *in toto*. Adults, when they're received into the church, have to say, as part of the rite of reception, that they "believe and profess all that the Holy Catholic Church believes, teaches and proclaims to be revealed by God." That is, the *receptandi* are asked to assent to the entire content of Catholic doctrine; they're asked to say that they agree that whatever the church teaches as doctrine in fact has that status. They aren't required to know all the particulars of that dogma; no one does, and if the *receptandi* were asked to, no one would ever be received into the church. Rather, they're asked to say that whatever it is that the church so defines, as revealed by the LORD, is in fact so revealed. They're asked, that is, to affirm an ecclesial faith, not to enumerate the dogmas and assent to them severally. And that this is so shows the centrality to the theological enterprise of discovering what in fact the church does teach on any theological question under consideration. This is important because the church, under the guidance and inspiration of the Holy Spirit, is a reliable teacher on matters of faith and morals. Dogmatic theology, therefore, discovering what the church teaches and trying to understand it, is essential to the theological task. The yield of such discovery is knowledge of truths about whatever is the theological topic at hand. The church's doctrine is the material with which theologians have to work—attending to it is what dogmatic theologians do—and part of the work of every Catholic theologian should be dogmatic in this sense.

Dogmatic theology, if done well, identifies with clarity and precision what the church bindingly teaches, and how gentle or harsh the bonds are in particular cases. The extent to which dogmatic theology is done well is also the extent to which clarity is reached about what the church doesn't teach—about, that is, what's left open for theological speculation in particular cases.

There is, for example, binding doctrine about what happens to the separated soul of a human creature at the body's death: Benedict XII's Constitution *Benedictus Deus* (1336) claims, among other things, that immediately upon (*mox*) the body's death, the separated soul enters purgatory or heaven or hell, and that these (preliminary) conditions find their last thing, their *novissimum*, only when souls are rejoined to bodies at the general resurrection. This is among the magisterial grounds for the non-negotiable Catholic affirmation of an intermediate state for human creatures between the body's death and their last thing. The discovery of dogma on this question entails discovery that there's no dogma, no binding teaching of any kind, about what the difference is between the heavenly vision of the LORD that belongs to separated souls in the intermediate state, and the heavenly vision of the LORD that belongs to embodied souls in heaven after the general resurrection. That's a question for speculation, a speculative question, as are all those on which there's no binding doctrine.

There is also binding doctrine, formulated and flagged exactly as such, on the question of Mary's assumption into heaven, body and soul together, which occurred, as the dogmatic definition, promulgated in 1950, has it, "when the course of her earthly life was completed" (*expleto terrestris vitae cursu*). But neither this definition nor any other specifies whether Mary died before she was assumed. The verbal formula is neutral to that question, and so it, too, is matter for speculation, a speculative question.

It is settled doctrine that the use of artificial contraceptive methods and devices is not licit. But there is no such settled doctrine even about exactly what counts as artificial, and much less about the acts and situations to which the ban applies. If we assume, as seems *prima facie* reasonable, that heterosexual intercourse provides the paradigm of such acts, then it's a question for speculation whether devices ordinarily used contraceptively in such acts can be used in acts that can't be contracepted because they are in principle not capable of resulting in conception—and if so, in which.

Calling theological questions whose answers aren't doctrinally determined "speculative" has a double sense. The first is exactly to flag that answers to them are not determined by what the church teaches. That fact doesn't locate the questions on an entirely open field: open fields are trackless and impossible to find your way about in. Even when no doctrinal answer is given to a question, the grammar of Catholic thought almost always suggests some tracks for thought to move along when considering it. That's certainly so in the cases of the intermediate state, Mary's death, and what counts as a licit means of contraception. Speculative theology, in this first sense of the word, is guided by doctrine, which is at least to say that the answers theologians offer to speculative questions have doctrinal resonance, and may enter into the church's future determinations of what is to count as doctrine.

The second sense of "speculative" has to do with mirrors. *Speculum* is a Latin word usually translated as "mirror." Following this etymology, speculative theologians are reflective in the ordinary sense of pausing to think; they also aim at the kind of reflectivity proper to mirrors. They hope, knowing they will fail, to see with perfect clarity the answer to the theological questions they're thinking about, and then to reflect what they've seen with the lack of distortion proper to a finely-ground mirror. They grind and polish the tools of thought—the distinction, the argument, the thought experiment, the counter-example—as a mirror-maker does glass, and with the same aim. They want to provide a flaw-less verbal artifact to those who might read or hear it.

To call some view or argument "speculative" can also (a third sense) suggest dubiousness, inconclusiveness, ungroundedness, and various other unpleasantnesses. This negative range of mean-ings is clearest when the word is used in financial contexts: specu-lation, when it fails, leads to ruin, and when it succeeds, to riches; in either case, it's a morally dubious bet. This sense of the word isn't in play here, and is worth noting only to stiff-arm.

Speculative and dogmatic theology need one another. The latter provides the former with the matter for its thought and argu-ment. The former suggests how the latter might be extended so that its meaning and implications become clearer to the church, to non-Christian theologians, and to pagan observers without theological inclinations. Catholic theologians, those who think, speak, and write about the LORD, need to know the difference between the two, and to practice both. The distinction informs all Catholic theological thinking, and its nature is one that all theologians would do well to keep in mind as one that ought to inform and structure their thought. The extent to which it fails to do those things is the extent to which thought fails to be properly Catholic-theological. Would-be theologians may fail in other ways as well (we all fail in many). But failure to observe and deploy the distinction between speculative and dogmatic theology is among the most common causes of failure to do Catholic theology—and perhaps of failure to do Christian theology of any variety.

§11 THEOLOGIANS

Theology requires theologians. The LORD has no need of theology except as an offering received, and unfallen angels are by nature too intimate with the LORD to need to do it. It's something we human creatures do, and (it's reasonable to assume) something that only we do. Which among us can do it? What qualifications or gifts or properties or capacities do theologians need? Since theology is a form of discourse whose goal is cognitive intimacy with the LORD about whom its practitioners speak and write, the short, simple, and correct answer to this question is that the qualifications necessary to be a theologian are only the necessary know-how (a matter of intellectual skill) coupled with sufficient knowledge-that (a matter of fluency produced by wide and deep reading in the tradition's archive). These qualifications aren't different from those needed for accomplishment in any intellectual discourse; with the appropriate changes in the particulars, they're just what's needed to become an economist or a literary critic or an historian. There's nothing mysterious about becoming and being a theologian: anyone with sufficient learning and skill can be; nothing more is required.

Catholic theology is a kind of discourse, differentiated from others by the fact that it's about the LORD in the mode of seeking cognitive intimacy, and by the fact that it's responsive to a particular set of theological authorities—namely, those affirmed as authoritative by the Catholic tradition. Those who produce Catholic theology—Catholic theologians—have talking and writing about the LORD as their characteristic activities. Performance of that sort is what theologians do. This understanding of theology and theologians is neutral with respect to attitude and affection.

Some theologians, certainly, love the LORD they think, talk, and write about: it seems reasonable to assume this of the saints, and of many non-saintly Catholic theologians. Others, though, hate that same LORD: even the demons believe, while hating and fearing the LORD they know, yet they are theologians too, and their understanding of the LORD is, because they are angels (fallen, but still angelic), in many respects more profound and intimate than that of human theologians. Yet other theologians neither hate nor love the LORD they think about. Some, perhaps, are like the Laodiceans, lukewarm in their loves, as devoted to the LORD they study as an historian of the American presidency might be to Grover Cleveland, or a historian of the English monarchy to George III; others, a more numerous tribe, are academically and distantly disinterested in the LORD. Most academic theologians are like this, skilled at their task, learned in its history, prolific in its discourse, dialectically precise in argument, and yet without love or hatred for the LORD about whom they write and talk. Thinking about the LORD can be a job of work, a *techne* with its own proper goods but without any necessary connection to the affections, or to the ordering and flourishing of a life.

So understanding the word "theology" is a minority view within the Catholic tradition. Most Catholics who have thought and written about the matter prefer a sense that, while acknowledging that theology is an intellectual *techne*, permits its practice only by those with qualifications additional to the intellectual. One way to effect such a restriction is to say that "theology" properly labels discourse about the LORD produced by the LORD's lovers, which entails that those who don't love the LORD while yet discoursing (even learnedly) about the LORD can't properly be called theologians. This disagreement is in large part semantic: it's about the extension—the range of reference—of "theology." But there's also at play in it, sometimes covert and sometimes overt, a disagreement about the nature and significance of love's knowledge, of what love makes it possible to know, and what its absence makes it impossible to know.

---

§12 LOVE'S KNOWLEDGE

Lovers of what they know have kinds and modes of intimacy with what they know unavailable to those who are not lovers. Lovers can, indisputably, know what it's like to love what they know; and, sometimes at least, their love opens to them aspects of, and even facts about, the beloved necessarily hidden from those without love. In the case of a human beloved, love's knowledge can go deep and range far. When I caress her, the caress may, if received as such, prompt a loving response revelatory of something about my beloved—her body, her face, her character, her thought, her speech—not given to those who do not caress and do not love her. My love for her may also impel me to attend to her more closely than I otherwise would, and in that way to come to know things about her that otherwise I wouldn't see.

The same two kinds of lover's knowledge may be available to lovers of the LORD: the LORD might show the LORD's face to his lovers in ways unavailable to others, rather as the LORD accepted Abel's sacrifice and refused Cain's; and those who love the LORD might be impelled to study the LORD and the LORD's ways to a degree they otherwise would not, and with an intensity that those who don't love the LORD are unlikely to have. There is a knowledge proper to love, and the extent that this is so is just the extent to which theologians who love the LORD are at a cognitive advantage over those who do not.

Love does not, however, provide only cognitive advantages. It may also bring blindnesses with it. That's obvious enough among humans. It may be that my beloved has faults to which I am blind but which are clearly evident to those who don't love her. The same is true even for human lovers of nonhuman creatures. If, for some hard-to-imagine reason, I had a deep devotion to the copperhead snake, I might as a result be insensitive to its dangers to humans, and might relate to specimens of it in ways that suggest blindness even to its dangers to me. Those who study it disinterestedly, or as an object of dislike or hatred, will come to know things about it that I do not. Love's knowledge is certainly different from indifference's or hatred's knowledge. But it isn't always, perhaps not even usually, greater in extent. Cognitive intimacies, for human creatures, are always limited in extent, and accompanied by particular blindnesses given by the concerns and interests of the knower. That's as true of love's knowledge as of other kinds.

Is it different with love for the LORD? The LORD, after all, has no faults to which lovers might be blinded by their love; and so, perhaps, love is an unmitigated advantage for aspiring theologians. Perhaps it yields only more cognitive intimacy and never less. But even this is not strictly true; those who know the LORD under the sign of hatred, whether they're fallen angels or humans, know something of the LORD that the LORD's lovers never can. They know the pain of willed separation, the burn of love deliberately refused, the scouring of the LORD's regret and anger at their lukewarmness or their hatred. They see the LORD's face under a different aspect than do lovers, but no less a true one. Theologians, then, need not be the LORD's lovers. They need only seek, and to the extent of their capacity find, cognitive intimacy with the LORD.

What about holiness? Sanctity isn't love; it's a settled state of intimacy with the LORD, inflected and interwoven with love, certainly, but different from it in tending toward indefectibility, and, in the case of the saints, in having arrived there. Might not sanctity be essential for cognitive intimacy with the LORD? Or at least helpful for it, contributory to and provocative of it, productive of it in ways that nothing else is? And haven't many in the church, including those with some magisterial authority, thought and taught just this? Yes; this is the majority view. And it's true that sanctity, like love, provides possibilities of knowing the LORD otherwise unavailable. But sanctity doesn't provide, or have anything much to do with, the cognitive skills necessary for knowing about the LORD, for arriving at the kind of intimacy with the LORD that theologians seek—which is to say cognitive intimacy. Some saints are stupid. Others, while not stupid, show little interest in the intellectual practices—making distinctions, offering arguments, imagining questions, burnishing thought experiments—necessary for cognitive intimacy with the LORD. Yet others among the saints are superlatively skilled at these things. But so are some who lack sanctity. Sanctity is, therefore, neither necessary nor sufficient for their acquisition. The Italian crone chattering at the cross (Newman's example) does know something more important than anything Aristotle knew. She knows Jesus. But she knows Jesus as does a lover or (perhaps) a saint. She doesn't know him as a theologian, or if she does it's not because she loves him. She would (let's assume) be less effective at glossing and interpreting the canons and decrees of the Council of Trent than many a half-trained pagan theologian and many a demonic curser of the LORD's name—who, after all, know that name well enough to curse it.

Perhaps, unlike sanctity, moral goodness is necessary for Catholic theologians, or at least useful for them. The moral virtues might permit theologians who have them to be conformed to Jesus more closely than those who lack them, and therefore to come to know him, and the triune LORD, better. Those virtues might even be necessary for good theology. Honesty, justice, courage, temperance, mercy—isn't a theologian with these better than one without them, and better not just as a person but also as a theologian? No. Certainly, these virtues are good to have, but they have nothing directly to do with the skills necessary for speaking and thinking well about the LORD. A man with only one leg lacks a good he'd be better off with, but that lack won't make him a worse (or better) theologian. Just so for a dishonest or cowardly theologian. There are and have been many good theologians whose moral character leaves much to be desired. Cyril of Alexandria, Jerome, Karl Barth, Paul Tillich, Martin Luther King, Jr.—these were, it seems likely, variously liars, plagiarists, adulterers, cholerically arrogant, and uncharitable. That didn't prevent them from thinking and writing well about the LORD; neither did it prevent them from writing and thinking better about the LORD than many theologians more morally virtuous than they.

Perhaps their moral vices prevented them from thinking as well about the LORD as they might have, assuming that their development of moral virtue didn't call into question or degrade their intellectual virtues. Maybe their moral vices served as partial obstructions to the perspicuity and profundity of their theological thinking. Maybe. But this, even if true (and its truth cannot, in concrete cases, be known), is contingently true in something like the same sense that quadriplegics might be better theologians if they weren't paralyzed because they'd have easier access to books. The state of theologians' bodies has the same kind of relation to their capacity to speak and write good theology as the state of their morals. Which is to say, not much in the order of being and nothing at all in the order of knowing: no one can easily tell from reading a theologian's work what the state of his or her life was, and it's unseemly to try. The attempt makes reading tea-leaves or entrails seem perspicuous.

This too is a minority position within the tradition. Most Catholics who've thought about the matter have approached, and sometimes affirmed, the position that a morally corrupt theologian is a contradiction in terms. This too is largely a lexical difference: "theology" is implicitly understood to label something good, and theologians are therefore thought to be of necessity good people. But it's hard to deny—and perhaps no one, when pressed, would—that bad people can think true things about the LORD, and once that's understood and instances of it produced (whether bad people can think true things about the LORD is best understood as an empirical question), the hard version of the majority position falls to the ground.

Even if it's true that love of the LORD, sanctity, and moral virtue are only contingently related to being a good theologian, isn't it also the case that Catholic theologians who've thought about the matter have typically insisted that the infused theological virtue of faith—not a moral virtue, not the same thing as holiness even if ingredient to it, and not the same thing as love of the LORD—is necessary for good theology, and perhaps even necessary for discourse about god (and the gods) to merit the modifier "Catholic," "Christian," or (even) "theological"? Perhaps so. If it is true it's because a certain kind of intimacy with the LORD can be received only as gift, and that intimacy yields a kind of knowledge of the LORD otherwise unavailable. And, if the infused theological virtue in question has baptism among its necessary conditions, then it follows that only Christians can do theology in the strict and proper sense of the word—or, to put the same point more precisely, that the modifier "Christian" in the phrase "Christian theology" has as much, perhaps more, to do with the identity of the theologian as with the content of the theology produced.

This family of views is deeply rooted and broadly scattered in the tradition; and it is coherently possible to restrict the meaning of "theology" in this way—that's a matter for stipulation. It's also possible that the kind of intimacy with the triune LORD given by baptism (another way of indicating the infused virtue of faith) might provide theological insights not otherwise available. But otherwise, and in every respect, this family of views ought be rejected by Catholic Christians. Christian theology—theology that knows and speaks of the triune and incarnate LORD in response to the history and authority that constitute Christianity and are recognized by Christians—can be, and is, done by the unbaptized. Catholic theology, that particular and most gorgeously full-bloomed variety of Christian theology, can be and is done by those out of full communion with the bishop of Rome. Not to think that these things are true is to embrace confusion and mystification. It's also to be blind to evidence: there's a great deal of theological talk and writing to hand in the world that bears on its face the marks of Christian (and Catholic) theology, and which is not spoken or written by the baptized.

---

§13 ECCLESIAL THEOLOGY

Baptism, together with a consequent and regular sacramental life; moral virtue; holiness; love of the LORD—these are all things good for anyone to have, and, consequently, good for those who write and talk about the LORD to have. But they have no intrinsic or proper connection to the production of such discourse. They are neither necessary nor sufficient for it; their presence provides only contingent aid for it and their absence only contingent obstruction. Even were there, in the order of being, such a connection, it doesn't, as a matter of observable fact, yield itself to observation. That is, even the most accomplished of theologians cannot, by reading the work of another theologian, ordinarily and easily arrive at reliable judgments about the baptismal status, sanctity, or moral virtue of the author. Again, it isn't seemly to try.

This view of theology's nature and the theologian's relation to the church does, though, seem to fly in the face of much in the tradition, and even some quite weighty magisterial texts. The theologian, it's often said, has an ecclesial vocation, and needs, therefore, to be intimate with the church and to recognize magisterial authority. Yes. But we need a distinction here. There certainly are ecclesial theologians in something like this sense, and the church has need of them. It's certainly possible to restrict the term "theologian" to them, and in some moods the teaching church and many of its speculative theologians do just that. But on this view what then to call those who write and speak about the LORD, whether in explicit response to what's been revealed by the LORD to the church (or in some broader sense), but who have no ecclesial vocation? The answer isn't obvious if the term "theologian" is banned for them, and the teaching church appears not to suggest or prescribe any answer to it, whether lexically or conceptually. In such a situation, the speculative Catholic theologian who does recognize the church's teaching authority is free to propose an extension in the meaning of the word "theology," together with its cognates and derivatives, so long as the conceptual distinction between the ecclesial theologian and others is preserved. And, in view of the lexical and conceptual confusion caused by refusing the status of theologian to the unbaptized, the vicious, and the less-than-holy, as well as the damage to the church's intellectual life caused by refusing to treat the writing and speech of such people as theological, "theology" is better understood with the meaning here given it. There are ecclesial theologians, certainly, and it would be good for the church, perhaps, if more theologians were ecclesial. But not all theologians are ecclesial, and the church needs the work and words of those who aren't, too, as its own history abundantly shows. There are things the church and its ecclesial theologians can learn from non-ecclesial theologians that it can't, in principle, learn from ecclesial theologians.

But why is it important to call what non-ecclesial, even pagan, theologians do "theology"? Doesn't that lead to confusion by suggesting an improper level of similarity, even of intimacy, between the work properly ecclesial "theologians" do and that of those who think about the LORD from without the church? Certainly the question of naming isn't the only or even the most fundamental question. It's more important to think and write about what it is that non-ecclesial theologians do than to argue about what to call it. But refusal to call what they do "theology" fosters blindness on the part of ecclesially Catholic theologians to its very existence. Lack of a name—and if what those who think and write about the LORD extra-ecclesially isn't to be called "theology," what is it to be called?—easily makes the nameless invisible, and among the needs that Catholic theologians have now, as always, is exactly the visibility, the strong presence, of extra-ecclesial theologians and their work.

Perhaps there's another objection to this line of thought. If we're considering what counts as Catholic theology, oughtn't we look at those who serve, for Catholic Christianity, as paradigmatic theologians? Wouldn't doing that show something important about what counts, and ought count, as Catholic theology? It would show something, certainly; those whom a tradition understands to be ideal-typical representatives of itself are indicative of its self-understanding in a deep way—as, perhaps, literature's Nobel laureates show something about what it is to be a person of letters, or winners of the Heisman trophy show something significant about what it is to be an amateur (American) football player. Good candidates for these paradigmatic figures in the case of

Catholic theology are the *doctores ecclesiae*, the church's teachers, declared by the church to have a "charism of wisdom bestowed by the Holy Spirit for the good of the Church," as Benedict XVI wrote in giving the title to John of Avila in 2012. These men and women, now numbering thirty-six, are baptized, judged to have lived holy lives and to be believers in and lovers of the LORD. Might this not suggest that all Catholic theologians ought be people of the church in these senses—and that the best theologians, those with the deepest and fullest insight into the LORD's nature, are all like that too?

No. Certainly, all those theologians who are baptized and who believe in and love the LORD ought seek sanctity—but that is true of all the baptized; nothing in it is specific or proper to the theologian's work or vocation. Certainly, too, love of the LORD may positively affect theological work, and did, so far as we can tell, in the case of the *doctores*. And of course the church looks to its own in seeking paradigms of theology and theologians. But the church also recognizes that the two things necessary for recognition as a *doctor ecclesiae*—eminence in doctrine and sanctity of life—are analytically separable. It's entirely possible to have one without the other, and eminence in one neither entails nor suggests anything about virtuosity in the other. There are theological errors and infelicities, and plenty of them, to be found in the work of the *doctores*; there are many not on the list of *doctores* whose skill at speaking and writing about the LORD exceeds that possessed and demonstrated by some of those who are on the list; and the list of *doctores* is not co-extensive with the list of the holiest people who have lived (it includes no martyrs, for example). What makes the *doctores* authoritative isn't their theology—their talk and writing about the LORD—alone. Neither is it their sanctity alone. Rather, it's their unusual combination of both, a combination whose rarity shows the separability of its components, coupled with the significance their theological work has accrued in the church's life over time. What belongs properly to the vocation of thinking, speaking, and writing about the LORD is the knowledge and skill that permit the practice. These do not include holiness of life, and the examples of the *doctores* do not show this to be otherwise.

Another way to put the possibility of non-ecclesial Catholic theology is to emphasize that the Catholic tradition has often distinguished intellectual from moral virtues, and both from theological virtues. These distinctions have sometimes been speculatively elaborated to a startling extent, as have the lists of particular virtues that belong to each category. Without engaging these elaborations, there's an obvious and useful application of the distinction between intellectual and other virtues to the topics under discussion here. The intellectual virtues are those habits proper to the engagement of intellectual topics; theology generally, and Catholic theology in particular, is a matter of and for the intellect; therefore the habits (virtues if they're good habits) appropriate to its practice are exactly the intellectual ones, whichever those turn out to be. And, since it's the case that inculcation and possession of intellectual virtues has not much to do with inculcation and possession of moral virtues—still less with theological ones—all that's necessary for the practice of Catholic theology is the particular intellectual habits appropriate to its performance.

But isn't this disputed? Don't some think that intellectual habits without their moral (and even theological) accompaniments are, somehow, not virtuous, and that good intellectual work, including good theological work, can therefore be done neither by those who aren't morally virtuous nor by those who lack the virtues that stem from baptism? It is disputed. It may even be a majority view among Catholics who've thought about this matter to say something like this. But the strategic and tactical disadvantages of holding this view are many; it is, on most definitions of the terms it deploys, manifestly false; and enough has been written already to suggest that this is so, and why. Morally vicious people can be intellectually brilliant; those who are deeply morally virtuous can be profoundly stupid; and the question of baptismal status has not much to do with either moral or intellectual virtue. What aspiring Catholic theologians need above all else is the right intellectual habits. With those in place, Catholic theology can be done; lacking them, it cannot.

---

§14 KNOWLEDGE, SKILL, FLUENCY

Those who would perform Catholic theology, where the adjective is understood to identify the discourse and its products rather than the identity or ecclesial location of the practitioner, need a body of knowledge and some particular skills. That's true of all discourses, and since Catholic theology is a discourse, it's true of it as well: knowledge-that and know-how, interwoven, are what make the performer able to perform. Since Catholic theological performance is an intellectual one, aimed at cognitive intimacy with the LORD, with verbal display as its characteristic artifact, the know-how needed for it is of the same sort as that needed for any intellectual performance. Theologians need to be as adept as they can become at formulating questions, making distinctions, offering arguments, rebutting objections, imagining thought experiments, and writing winsomely lucid prose. That's true of all intellectual workers; these are the tools of the trade, and those who (want to) do Catholic theology need them as much as anyone else.

There's always also a grammar, comprising a more-or-less specialized lexicon and some more-or-less complex syntactical rules. Fluency in this grammar is tightly indexed to capacity to make a contribution to the theological enterprise, and in the case of a complex grammar with a long history, fluency is always a hard-won skill, never capable of final mastery or anything like comprehension. Know-how just is skill, a formal capacity; but it's always inextricably linked with a body of knowledge that such-and-such is the case. Often, this body of knowledge is to hand in an archive, a collection of texts; the archive may be important intrinsically—that is, its extent and content may itself be what the performer needs to know. Or, it may be important extrinsically, for what it claims. The Catholic archive is important in both ways. The Catholic theologian needs to know its extent and nature, as well as the claims it makes upon the theologian and about the LORD and the world. Coming to know the archive—reading it extensively and intensively, with guidance and under instruction—is also the principal way in which the tradition's grammar is learned. Knowing-how and knowing-that merge at this point.

---

§15 THE CATHOLIC ARCHIVE

The Catholic archive is extensive. Its earliest constituents approach three millennia in age—they are the oldest texts of the Old Testament. Its most recent belong to today. Geographically, too, there's a broad spread. The Mediterranean basin is the place where most of the archive's artifacts were made in the early centuries, but more recent centuries have seen them be produced almost everywhere on the planet. Rome, though, historically and still now, is the geographic center of the archive, the place toward which all its artifacts are oriented. The archive is, in its own self-understanding and self-presentation, largely a matter of the word, and is found, therefore, paradigmatically in texts, among which the canon of scripture is archetypically and foundationally authoritative. Every other artifact, textual and otherwise, resonates with and to this one, and that's because scripture is *verbum Domini*, the LORD's word.

The archive, however, is not only or merely verbal. It contains paintings, statues, buildings, relics of the bodies of the Christian dead, liturgical implements, clothing, musical scores, and much more—artifacts intended to engage all the senses. Most of what Catholics do and make in response to the LORD's gifts passes away, from a human point of view, as soon as it comes into being. This is true of speech and music and the movements of bodies in space and the rising of incense smoke to the LORD; and so these things, though they belong to the archive in a sense (they are present now as always to the LORD), are not accessible for study or use once they have passed away. But a small portion remains, and some artifacts are preserved and handed on intentionally because they're taken to be essential to or important for the archive. The Catholic theologian ought, ideally, be conversant with and responsive to the preserved archive in its entirety, but that is impossible for any individual because the archive is too extensive. It's a more reasonable aspiration that the corpus of Catholic theologians as a whole be conversant with the whole archive, which means that theology—the performance of discourse about the LORD—must, therefore, be a collaborative and consultative enterprise.

The Catholic archive is Catholic theologians' data. It's what's given to us, that upon which we work. The artifacts we aim to produce, like the heart of the archive itself, are verbal. Theologians' focus, therefore, ought also be unremittingly verbal. Our training is verbal/grammatical: what we do is verbal/grammatical; and the divine-human person Jesus, who is the Christ, the axis and heart

of the tradition, is himself the Word and syntax of the created order—he, too, is verbal/grammatical. We theologians are creatures
of this Word, and the words he has provoked. This ought always
be at the heart of our self-understanding, and of the means we use
to burnish our theological skills. To be a Catholic theologian is,
first and last, to be a speaker and writer of words about the triune
LORD whose incarnation is verbal.

The Catholic archive cannot be mastered by any theologian.
That is for at least two reasons. The first is that the archive is too
extensive. No one person can have acquaintance with anything
but a small portion of it. Choices must be made and the gaze
must be focused. This is a practical necessity. The second reason
is more pressing. It is that what lies at the heart of the tradition,
and what Catholic theology is explicitly about, is the living LORD
who cannot be comprehended—and therefore also not mastered—in concept or reality. The concept of the LORD is of a simple but triune one who is the donor of being and who is incarnate.
This is a concept that stretches concepts to the point of breakage.
It is capable of only formal or tentative analysis. Were it not of that
kind, it wouldn't be a concept of the LORD, but rather of a creature. This is as true for the lovers of the LORD as for those who
hate or are indifferent to the LORD; the concept does the same
conceptual work for all who entertain it. And in reality, for those
who assent and respond to the LORD's reality, incomprehensibility and unmasterability are intrinsic to what they respond to. We
do not pray to someone or something we might master.

The Catholic archive provides the content of what Catholic
theologians need to know. It does this not contingently but essentially: it contains the verbal record—in the case of the textual archive—of the LORD's dealings with and instructions to the people
the LORD has chosen. Attending to the archive is essential for
the theologian not only because it provides the lexicon and syntax

of Catholic speech, and not only because it yields (partial) knowledge about the LORD, but also because it contains the church's progressively developed understanding of what the LORD has given to her, and this understanding cannot be bypassed in order to arrive at the truth by some route imagined to be more direct. A theologian who did that, or tried it, would be like a wife who knew what could be known of her husband, but who had forgotten—by refusing to attend to—their history together. The history of Catholic theology is not incidental to its content, and so the theologian must attend to the archive which contains that history.

§16 SCRIPTURE, CANON, *VERBUM DOMINI*

The fundamental and central feature of the Catholic archive is the canon of scripture. It didn't come first in the order of making. The people of Israel were called into existence long before there was a Tanakh, and the church existed for a long time before, in response to the Spirit's guidance, it collected and closed the canon of the New Testament. Scripture is therefore not a necessary condition for the existence of either Christians or Jews. Both have existed without it, and will again: it is part of the grammar of Christian orthodoxy to say that scripture belongs to the devastation only; it had no place in paradise and will have none in heaven. Once it comes into being in the devastation, however, it has a significance for Catholic theology of a different order than any other component of the archive. We read it at every liturgy; we identify it when we do so as *verbum Domini*, the LORD's word; we endlessly return to it as an object of commentary, argument, exegesis, and contemplation; we represent its scenes and stories in painting and statuary; we set its events to music; and we tell it to our children.

We do some of these things with other bodies of texts from the archive, and with other artifacts from it; but in no other case do we combine them with as we do with scripture. Scripture is *sui generis* because it and it alone is given to us by the LORD as his words to us in the post-Babel languages we use. Every Catholic theologian must know and use it, even if not all to the same extent and in the same way. Theology without scripture would be like the English language without verbs—clauseless and incommunicado.

What is the canon of scripture? Which are its words? Where are they to be found? These aren't easy questions to answer. Scripture is not to be found in any one natural language. The Old Testament does not exist only, or even paradigmatically, in Hebrew or Aramaic, even though these were the languages in which the texts that together constitute it were composed. Likewise, the New Testament doesn't exist only or paradigmatically in Greek, even though that is the language in which its component texts were composed (there are some outcroppings of Aramaic in this Greek sea, present there as quotations or names; but otherwise, everything in the New Testament was composed in Greek). No. The right picture is that the canon of scripture contains seventy-three component texts, forty-six in the Old Testament and twenty-seven in the New; that these, taken together, with the division between those that belong to the Old and those that belong to the New clearly marked and in the order established by the church, are what the canon of scripture is; and that this canon is available to Catholics as the LORD's word—as *verbum Domini*—in any and every version approved for public liturgical reading by the church, which is to say, as things are in the church now, by local synods of bishops with the power to make such determinations. The canon of scripture, the LORD's words to the chosen people, is fully available, unveiled and without occlusion, in all the versions in all the languages in which the church at any time reads and proclaims it at worship. It is available, therefore, in Latin, Greek, English, French, Japanese, Spanish, Swahili, Tagalog, Xhosa, and very many more. None is privileged and none excluded. The church has no sacred language, no natural language more intimate with what the LORD has said than any other. That is among the Catholic church's distinctive features; the exegetical practices of most Protestants imply that only the scriptural texts in the language of their composition are really scripture; and Jews, for the most part, think that Hebrew is more intimate with the LORD's speech than any other language. Views like these aren't proper to Catholicism (they have other drawbacks, too).

At Babel, as the account in Genesis has it, the variety of natural languages came into being, with their mutual incompatibility and incomprehensibility, as a curse. Before that there had been one, paradisial language, comprehensible to all fully and without obstruction. The curse of Babel was reversed at Pentecost, but not by reconstituting the paradisial language, or by bringing into being some new language, Esperanto-like, that all could understand. Rather, the Spirit made it possible for all those listening to what the inspired disciples of the ascended Jesus were saying to them to hear and understand what was being said in their mother tongue, their local vernacular. This is the charter for the deep, almost obsessive, Christian interest in translation; it is what makes it impossible for Catholic Christians to have a sacred language, or to think that the canon of scripture in any one natural language— even the language of its composition—is privileged, somehow more the LORD's word than (translated) versions in other languages. When the scriptural book is read from at worship and flagged as the LORD's word to the people, it belongs to Catholic orthodoxy to judge that this is really so. An English or Spanish version of scripture isn't a pale and inadequate reflection of something else, something Greek or Hebrew, which is the real word of the LORD. No. Every version of scripture authorized by the church to be read and proclaimed as the LORD's word really and fully is that, without reservation.

Doesn't this mean that the canon of scripture becomes enormously large? That the words which make it up are almost uncountable, and that they include words in hundreds of languages, perhaps thousands? Yes. Exactly. This conclusion follows from the church's liturgical habits. The LORD addresses the people through the words of scripture in all the languages they speak; and this address is of the same kind no matter what the language being used. It also means that the set of words that makes up the canon of scripture varies over time—that as a translation is made into some language in which scripture hasn't previously been available, and then authorized by a local synod of bishops for liturgical reading and proclamation in their region, the corpus of scriptural texts grows; and that when a scriptural version previously authorized ceases to be so, or as the last speaker of some language dies and no one is any longer capable of reading that version, the corpus of scriptural texts contracts. The canon of scripture is fixed and invariant in one way: it consists of just and only its component seventy-three books, with their particular histories of composition, translation, canonization, and use. But in another way it is not fixed at all: like a symphonic score, scripture can be performed in endlessly new languages, and in endlessly new settings and styles, as the Spirit leads. The extent of the canon is an opportunity for exegetes, and an instance of the LORD's radical excess as a giver. Scripture isn't given once for all as a frozen collection of Hebrew and Greek texts; it's constantly regiven, without withholding, whenever scripture is read as *verbum Domini* in the hearing of the baptized.

It seems that, on this view, there can be no such thing as a mistranslated or badly translated version or piece of scripture. If it suffices for a version to be canonically scriptural that it receive episcopal approval, then mistranslations and other infelicities can easily become part of the scriptural canon. There are notorious examples—Romans 5:12 as found in (most) versions of the Vulgate is a bad rendering of the Greek version of that verse. Won't it be the case that incompatible renderings of particular parts of scripture might all belong to the canon, and isn't this unacceptable, a *reductio ad absurdum*?

Certainly this is an entailment of the position here sketched. If there's no court of appeal beyond episcopal authority and liturgical practice for the establishment of what counts as (an instance of) the canon of scripture, then all these things may happen—and have happened. But the church has confidence in the Spirit's capacity to guide it, as well as in the capacity, limited and damaged though it is, of its bishops and people to recognize and respond to that guidance. That recognition and response are evident in the development of ecclesial understanding of what does and what should count as (an instance of) the canon of scripture. As doctrine develops over time, not in a smooth upward curve toward full and perfect and final understanding, but rather in a jagged line, running upwards in fits and starts with halts and diversions and *culs-de-sac* recognizable only retrospectively, so also for the church's ability to recognize what does and what does not belong properly to the expanding and contracting content of the canon. First-blush incompatibilities of a semantic sort among translated versions of the scriptural canon are an exegetical opportunity as much as they're a problem, and they're a more comprehensive opportunity when the problem looks at first to be deep, even irresolvable. They're not different in this respect from the first-blush incompatibilities within a particular version of the scriptural canon, and those have been and remain among the principal engines of doctrinal development. The best response by theologians to the expanding and contracting thesaurus of scripture is gratitude and intellectual excitement for the theological opportunities it affords.

There's another significant difficulty with this putatively Catholic view of the scriptural canon. It appears to remove authority from the originals, from the untranslated versions composed in Hebrew, Aramaic, and Greek. Can this be defensible? Isn't there by now a long Catholic tradition of attributing primacy exactly to these originals? No. The originals have primacy in some senses, but not in all. They have primacy in the sense that they came first: the translations depend upon them, and not the other way around. They also have primacy in the sense that, unlike all the other versions, which are translations, the relation they bear to the version they're translating cannot be studied because there is no such version and therefore no such relation. But they have no primacy as *verbum Domini*, and, therefore, also no primacy as sources for determining the content of that word or as material for proclaiming that word to the people. Both the church's liturgical practice and its magisterial teaching make this position something very close to church doctrine. It follows from this position that the disproportionate attention paid by Catholic exegetes since the mid-twentieth century to the untranslated versions of scripture is misplaced. What a Latin or Cantonese or Swahili version of scripture contains is just as revelatory and just as theologically suggestive as what a Greek or Hebrew version contains. The translated versions need study and commentary just as much as the untranslated ones.

The canon is linguistically multiple in the sense that it's available in many natural languages. It's literarily single in that every instance of it in every language contains just the same books in just the same order. A principal and important difference between Catholics and Protestants is evident in these matters. Protestants are more likely than Catholics to think the untranslated versions of scripture have a different order of revelatory authority than do translated versions, difficult though it is to sustain such a view and make it coherent with (even Protestant) ecclesial practice. Most Protestants also have an incomplete canonical collection: their list of the books that comprise the Old Testament typically contains only thirty-nine items because, with very few exceptions, they follow the canonical list (though not the order) of the books found in the Jewish Tanakh as closed and frozen by the Masoretes. Catholics, by contrast, follow the older, longer (and also Jewish) list of books given in the Septuagint, the pre-Christian rendering into Greek, by Jews for Jews, of what Christians would later come to call the Old Testament. These differences are among the deeper roots of the separation between Catholics and Protestants.

Every Catholic theologian needs to be as intimate with the canon of scripture as possible. That's because all Catholic theological discourse ought be responsive to scripture, resonant with what the canon says and how it says it. Scripture ought to be a constant interlocutor for all Catholic theologians. Doesn't that place an impossible burden on Catholic theologians? We can't all become scripture scholars. That academic specialty is more than a life's work—Greek, Hebrew, Syriac, Coptic, together with an ocean of secondary, scientific scholarship. Even those who would self-describe as scholars of scripture eschew intimacy with the whole canon; they specialize, instead, in this or that piece of it (the synoptics, the prophets, the wisdom literature), and write monographs on this or that pericope. Shouldn't Catholic theologians restrict themselves to what they do best, which is to speak and write about the LORD?

It's true that not all Catholic theologians need to undertake technical exegetical work on the untranslated versions of scripture. It's also the case that not much of the self-designated scientific exegetical work on these versions is of any use for theological enterprises. But to identify the use of scripture for theological purposes with those undertakings is a cramped view of how scripture may be used by theologians. Better to say that intimacy with the canon in one or more of its versions ought be a part of the ordinary equipment of Catholic theologians; that absence of serious engagement with scripture should be understood as a serious lack whenever it occurs; and that Catholic theologians whose library (material or virtual) does not include scripture in several versions, often consulted, lacks something essential. Not all Catholic theological discourse need be explicitly engaged with scripture to the same extent; but it does all need to be responsively formed by the canon.

§17 PARTICULAR VERSIONS OF SCRIPTURE

Catholic Christianity has no sacred language and is committed to the idea that the LORD's word can be made fully available in any natural language, and that it ought be made available in as many as possible. But the history of Christianity has given some versions of scripture a special status because of their long and widespread use. First among those versions is the Vulgate, the Latin version of the canon in common (hence "Vulgate") use in Europe and its environs and offshoots for more than a thousand years. This version had its origin in Jerome's work in the late fourth and early fifth centuries; he wanted to improve and standardize the various older Latin versions of the Old and New Testaments then in circulation, and he did this by providing fresh Latin renderings made directly from Hebrew of some parts of the Old Testament, and by revising extant Latin versions of parts of the New Testament with an eye to the Greek. Subsequent work, by Jerome and others, eventually led to something close to a standard Latin text of the entire canon for the West. There was never a finally fixed text, not even after printed editions began to be produced. But the Latin text that was read, commented on, proclaimed, expounded, illustrated, and ornamented throughout Europe between the fifth and fifteenth centuries was close enough to common and fixed that it makes sense to think of it and treat it as a single version. It is the version quoted and presupposed by all Latin-using preachers, canonists, bishops, popes, and theologians for a thousand years, and for that reason alone every Catholic theologian needs a copy and needs to consult it and read in it often.

For theologians whose Latin is good enough easily to read in or consult the text of the Vulgate, but who are unlikely to do, or want to know about, specialized text-critical work, the best and most usable edition is the one-volume *Biblia Sacra Iuxta Vulgatam Versionem*, published by the Deutsche Bibelgesellschaft beginning in 1969. The most recent (fifth) edition appeared in 2007. For the English-user whose Latin is more dubious, an excellent resource is the seven-volume facing-page Latin-English edition of the Vulgate published by the Dumbarton Oaks Medieval Library under the editorship of Swift Edgar and others between 2010 and 2013. This has the advantage of providing the Douay-Rheims English version of scripture, whose first version was begun in 1582 and completed in 1610. Extensive revisions to it were made in the mid-eighteenth century, and for almost three centuries various editions of this version, a closely literal rendering of the (so-called) Sixto-Clementine edition of the Vulgate, were the only English versions of scripture approved by the church for liturgical use in the English-speaking world. The Douay-Rheims has almost no literary merit: it sacrifices just about everything English (euphony, syntax, rhetoric, flavor, and even, sometimes, comprehensibility) to intimacy with the Latin it tries to reflect. But it does provide an essential window into the English-speaking Catholic world from the late sixteenth to the early twentieth century. Use of the Dumbarton Oaks edition, therefore, is close to essential for the English-speaking and English-writing Catholic theologian.

Catholic theologians ought also have to hand the text of the *Nova Vulgata*, or New Vulgate. This is an extensive revision of the Vulgate's text set in motion by Paul VI in 1965 with the goal of providing a common Latin text that might be the principal point of reference in the continuing work of revising the church's liturgical books, and that might also reflect some of the advances made in establishing a (Latin) text of scripture. Work was done on this revision for more than twenty years, and the authoritative *editio typica* was published at Rome in 1986, as *Nova Vulgata Bibliorum Sacrorum Editio*. The Latin text found in this edition differs in some significant and many insignificant ways from that given in the (old) Vulgate, almost always in the direction of intimacy with the Hebrew (for the Old Testament) and Greek (for the New). This New Vulgate is now the text printed in the authoritative Latin editions of the church's liturgical books—the lectionary for mass, both Sunday and daily, as well as the books that contain the liturgy of the hours, the church's daily office. This means, or probably means, that as revisions and new versions of these liturgical books in the vernacular are made, the New Vulgate will come to have a greater impact on the church's intellectual as well as its liturgical life. Catholic theologians therefore need to have this version of scripture to hand for reading and consultation.

Catholic theologians should also consult and read in the more important among the local vernacular versions of scripture. For theologians working in the United States in the twenty-first century, for example, this means at least the New American Bible, which is the English version of scripture approved for liturgical use by the U.S. Catholic bishops at the moment. It means also the other English versions, Catholic, Protestant, or Orthodox, important locally for scholarly or historical reasons—in the United States these include the King James (Authorized) version for its historical importance; the Revised Standard and New Revised Standard versions (there are Catholic editions of these) for their wide use across ecclesial boundaries; and the New International Version for its wide use in broadly evangelical Protestant communities. It should include also the New Jerusalem Bible because of its use, liturgical and scholarly, in English-speaking parts of the world outside the United States.

The text of the Septuagint (LXX) should also be part of the Catholic theologian's library. It's reasonable to think of this as the earliest version of the canon of the Old Testament, and as the version most often quoted in the texts of the New. Both these claims (over)-simplify a complicated story—"Septuagint" is an umbrella-term for a family of Greek versions of the Old Testament, and there is no univocally simple answer to the question of which versions of the Old Testament the writers of the New used. But they serve as useful generalizations. They serve also to indicate the importance of the Septuagint for the Christian tradition generally and for Catholics in particular. Serious analysis of and response to New Testament texts, especially, inevitably involves reference to the Septuagint.

Manual editions of the untranslated versions of scripture are also important to have at hand—Hebrew (and Aramaic) for the Old Testament, and Greek for the New. Reliable editions of these are easy to come by. If the theologian can easily read them, so much the better. If not, they're important for reference: sometimes it's relevant to the formulation and analysis of theological questions to consider a translation-chain—for example, the relations between the rendering of a New Testament passage in English,

Latin, and Greek; or the connections between a New Vulgate version of an Old Testament passage and the version found in the (Hebrew) Masoretic text. These untranslated versions, even though they're no more or less significant as the LORD's word than any other, have a pervasive historical and scholarly significance which the theologian often needs to know about and engage.

But isn't this also a counsel of perfection? Few Catholic theologians in the English-speaking world have facility in Hebrew, Aramaic, Greek, and Latin; fewer have any sense of the current scholarly state of play in textual or interpretive questions about scripture. The program suggested approaches asking all theologians also to be scholars of scripture. That will divert them from their real task, which is exactly to do theology, not to provide scriptural exegesis. That should be left to the scripture scholars.

There certainly are technical questions that ought be left to them. Theologians, as theologians, can't contribute to text-critical questions about scripture and shouldn't try; the same is often true about particular historical questions. But what's being suggested here is not the acquisition and exercise of expertise of those kinds. Rather, it's knowledge of the contours and content of the canon in the versions most historically and locally important for the practice of Catholic theology—that, for the North American English-speaking theologian means knowledge and use of the Septuagint, the Vulgate, the New Vulgate, the Douay-Rheims, the New American Bible, and a scattering of other significant English versions. It means also consultation as occasion demands of the Hebrew/Aramaic Old Testament and the Greek New. That's neither impossible nor burdensome: a dozen volumes on the shelf, together with a half-dozen more works of reference (concordances, dictionaries) makes it all available, within arm's length. Scripture is a fundamental and central part of the archive, and Catholic theologians ought be serious about engaging it. What's recommended here is minimal; more may be needed for particular theological questions, but this is certainly not too much.

§18 CONCILIAR TEXTS

The Catholic archive is fundamentally scriptural, but is neither exclusively nor predominantly so. Another component of it, essential for Catholic theologians, is the texts promulgated by the bishops in synod at the twenty-one ecumenical, or general, councils recognized by Catholics as authoritative. The first of these was held at Nicaea in 325, and the last (for the moment) at Rome (the Second Vatican Council) from 1962 to 1965. These texts are authoritative, according to the grammar of the faith, because they are the collective voice of all the church's teachers—its bishops—gathered in one place and speaking in unison under the guidance of the Spirit to the church and the world. That's the internal position. Looked at externally, by those who recognize neither the Spirit's guidance nor, therefore, episcopal authority, the account that belongs to the faith's grammar looks naive and unjustifiable: it's never the case that all the bishops gather, or that they all agree. But even from that point of view, it remains true that Catholic theology as a kind of discourse does have these texts as authoritative elements of its archive, and that a theology (or a theologian) that prescinded from them could not be fully Catholic.

The texts from the ecumenical councils are not all of one kind, and not all of equal significance for the theological task. Some, mostly called canons, are administrative or disciplinary; they speak to ecclesial and political situations long past. These, while important and sometimes theologically suggestive, belong for the most part to the historian rather than the theologian. The most weighty and the most important for the theologian are the decrees, sometimes pastoral and sometimes doctrinal, but always authoritative and often determinative of doctrine. When considering any theological topic, Catholic theologians need to ask whether there is anything relevant to be found among these decrees. Frequent reference to and reading in them is an essential and distinctive part of the Catholic theologian's work; other Christian theologians recognize fewer than twenty-one ecumenical councils, and some recognize none. The Catholic archive is richer and fuller than others, and is more fully articulated with the history of the tradition.

For the English-using theologian, the most convenient manual edition of the conciliar texts is the two-volume edition by Norman Tanner and others under the title, *Decrees of the Ecumenical Councils*. This is a facing-page edition, with the original-language texts (mostly Latin, but some Greek and the occasional outcropping of Syriac) on verso, and English on recto. These volumes ought always be within theologians' reach as they do their work.

The question of the authoritative weight of translated versions of conciliar texts is a complex one; in the case of English renderings, there are often several different ones in circulation, and there is no very clear means of determining which, if any, has received formal ecclesial approval. The theologians' rule of thumb here is to take the untranslated versions as authoritative, and translated versions as trots and teaching tools. This rule of thumb has the double advantage of underlining the difference between the authority borne by scripture and that borne by the decrees of the ecumenical councils, and of being in broad accord with the church's practice of appealing to and using the conciliar decrees.

§19 MAGISTERIAL TEXTS

The church is a teacher, a *magister*, principally because its bishops are led by the Spirit into a fuller understanding of what the LORD has revealed in scripture and given to the church. This doesn't mean that individual bishops are beyond error, or even that bishops gathered in local synod are so. Only the bishop of Rome formulating doctrine *ex cathedra*, from the episcopal authority-seat, is beyond error in that way, and such formulations and promulgations are vanishingly rare. Though they aren't beyond error, sometimes widespread and deep-going, the idea that the bishops are Spirit-led does mean that the teachings they give, whether as individuals instructing their priests and people, or in local and trans-local assembly, have weight. The formulation and promulgation of such teaching contributes to the archive as ornament to and elaboration of the deposit of faith. It ought be consulted and responded to by theologians.

It isn't easy to say just what belongs to this constituent of the archive. Attempting to define its limits provides a theological discussion without final resolution if what's being sought are necessary and sufficient conditions. But there are clear cases, and, thus, good rules of thumb. When a local (usually, these days, national) synod of bishops meets and offers teaching, Catholic theologians who live and work in the jurisdiction ought take what's promulgated seriously. They need to know what their bishops are teaching and have taught. For example, Catholic theologians in the United States considering how to think theologically about the movement of peoples across national boundaries ought include in the material with which they have to work the public teachings of the U.S. Catholic bishops on this matter. This material isn't all of the same kind. Some is merely advisory; some is more or less transient, as when a representative of the bishops offers evidence and recommendations to one or another agency of the U.S. legislature or judiciary; and some is more formal or long-lasting, consisting of attempts to enunciate and elaborate the grammar of Catholic thinking about the topic. Different degrees of *obsequium religiosum* (religious submissiveness) on the part of Catholic theologians to such local episcopal teachings are appropriate to different elements of it, and it is part of the theological task to assess and properly respond to what the bishops provide. This means, in turn, that theologians need to know, refer to, and gratefully consult the body of teachings provided by their local bishop and their local synod. Different localities have different means of making such material available. It's part of the theologian's task to know what these are, and thus to keep abreast of this part of the archive. Just as it's the habit of some Catholics to kiss their bishop's ring when they meet him, in recognition of and gratitude for his authority, so theologians should kiss the textual body of local episcopal teaching. It's something good to have, a conversation partner delightful to talk with.

The body of magisterial teaching has universal as well as local elements. The bishops teach in various ways and in various genres—by bull, by encyclical, by apostolic letter and advice, in audience, in homilies, in pastoral instructions of various kinds, in addresses to secular bodies, and so on—and even, on occasion, in speculative theology done in their own names rather than in the name of their episcopal office. Their teaching is communicated to the universal church in equally varied ways. This body of teaching, too, should be gratefully received, studied, known, and, when relevant to their theological projects, taken seriously by Catholic theologians. Papal teaching, too, like all episcopal teaching, is not all of one kind or all of the same authoritative weight. Some, certainly, is formally doctrinal or disciplinary, and therefore weighty as a contribution to the formation of the church's thought on this or that topic. Much, though, is occasional, pastoral, ephemeral, and local, which doesn't make it less interesting and suggestive, but does make it less binding. Regular consultation of *Acta Apostolica Sedis* (Acts of the Holy See), which is the title of the journal of record for these matters since 1909, together with *L'Osservatore Romano* in one or another of its many vernacular versions will keep theologians abreast of the scope and ebb and flow of papal teachings.

§20 DENZINGER

An essential work of reference for the deposit of magisterial teaching is what's familiarly called "Denzinger," after Heinrich Denzinger (1819–83), the editor of the first edition (1854) of (what's now called) *Enchiridion symbolorum definitionum et declarationum de rebus fidei et morum* (Compendium of Creeds, Definitions, and Declarations on Matters of Faith and Morals). The work contains what its title suggests. It's a florilegium, arranged chronologically, of professions of faith, conciliar documents, papal teachings, and material from local synods. Each extract is presented in the language of its first, and authoritative, promulgation, which is typically also the language of its composition. Denzinger is not comprehensive in its coverage of any of the kinds of material it presents—for conciliar documents, for example, it should be supplemented by Tanner's edition—but it does bring together a wide range of the church's teachings on all the major doctrinal topics, and it has the advantage of having been, since 1854, the most widely-used reference of its kind and, therefore, of having shaped not only the transmission of the church's teaching, but also the formulation of its doctrine.

Denzinger's chronological arrangement, combined with its intended use as a work to be consulted for the church's teaching on particular doctrinal topics, requires extensive subject-indexing; consultation of the development of these indices in the successive editions of Denzinger over time shows a great deal about how the shape of Catholic theology has been understood and presented over time. In its most recent edition (the forty-third was published in 2010; it covers material through 2008, the third year of Benedict XVI's papacy; new editions appear approximately every decade) Denzinger ought be on hand for, and often in the hands of, all Catholic theologians.

Denzinger is itself part of the archive, but an idiosyncratic one. It is almost exclusively an anthology of elements of the archive, and so its contribution to the archive isn't the provision of words not previously there, but rather that of selection and arrangement of material already in the archive. It shapes the archive and gives the church and its theologians habits of approaching and using it. There are dangers for theologians in using it. Denzinger's arrangement can suggest that every element of it is equally authoritative, just as every definition in a dictionary can be taken to have equal weight; but so taking the elements of Denzinger would itself be an offense against the grammar of Catholic faith. Also, the fact that Denzinger usually does not provide complete texts but rather extracts means that doctrinal positions can seem plausible which would seem much less so were the complete document to hand. Using Denzinger properly requires skill and knowledge extrinsic to itself, and in ways that go deeper and are less obvious than is the case for most texts. None of these caveats, however, lessens Denzinger's importance for the work of Catholic theology.

§21 CATECHISMS AND CREEDS

To catechize is to provide instruction. The Greek verb (*katecheo*) that underlies the English word means "to cause [someone] to hear [something]," and so the root meaning of the word has to do with oral instruction. This is the sense that Augustine had in mind when, early in the fifth century in North Africa, he composed a work called *De catechizandis rudibus* (Catechizing the Uninstructed) —the catechetical scene he imagined in that text was oral and face-to-face. (In Latin, as in English, the Greek word is calqued; it appeared to Latin eyes as much of an alien intrusion as "catechesis" and "catechize" do to English ones.) Soon enough, though, catechisms became texts, handy compendia of doctrine (and sometimes other information) used for the education of children, the preparation of adults for baptism and confirmation, and the training of priests. Such texts typically organize the matter of Christian doctrine according to some easily-recognizable scheme (the petitions of the Lord's Prayer, the ten commandments, the seven gifts of the Spirit, and so on), are divided into brief sections—little flowers—suitable for brief, daily study sessions, and are sometimes given in question-and-answer form as a textual trace of their oral origins and to facilitate memorization and testing of their content. Catholic and Protestant Christians have made much use of catechisms as a textual genre; Orthodox Christians rather less.

A catechism is a creed writ large. The latter, from *credo*, "I believe," or *credimus*, "we believe," are concentrated statements, typically a few dozen words in length, and never more than a few hundred. The so-called Apostles' Creed numbers 110 words in the English version currently used by Catholics in North America; the Nicene-Constantinopolitan Symbol 224 words; and even such

rarely-used quasi-creeds as the Quicumque Vult, the so-called
Athanasian Creed, do not much exceed five hundred words.
Creeds are meant to be memorized and recited aloud and (usually) in unison in public worship; their principal setting is liturgical,
and they are typically too compressed to be easily understood by
themselves. They presuppose and suggest a relaxed and expansive
instruction which they do not themselves provide. That's what catechisms give. Those are often long—the (1992) *Catechism of the
Catholic Church* runs to almost nine hundred pages in its printed
editions—and while some among them were meant to be used
in part as memorizable call-and-response texts, they are mostly
too long to make memorization easily possible. Creeds are kept in
the memory to be recited at call; catechisms are kept on the shelf
to be consulted at need. But they both serve a similar purpose: to
schematize and summarize Christian doctrine in such a way as to
make it available and usable.

What use are creeds and catechisms to the aspiring or practicing Catholic theologian? If credal recitation is principally a liturgical matter, and the composition and use of catechisms principally
a pedagogical one, aimed at unsophisticated and uneducated
Christians—Augustine's *rudes*—then surely they don't have much
to tell the theologian. Such things are, perhaps, to theologians'
tasks as alphabet-books are to novelists'. It's true that creeds and
catechisms don't contain much speculative theology. It's also true
that they're didactic rather than argumentative, stipulative rather
than subtle. Nonetheless, theologians need them. They provide,
first, important data. They show how the church has, at various
times and in various places, understood the shape and content of
its doctrine, and this is essential knowledge for theologians. That's
as true for theologians who believe in and love the LORD they
speak and write about as it is for those who don't. An approximate
analogy: the authorities charged with applying relevant law to

those seeking immigration into the United States provide study materials to aspiring Americans; they're tested on them, and, in some cases, expected to memorize elements of them. These materials aren't discursively extended, and aren't argumentative or speculative. They organize and present facts—or putative facts—about the American polity's structure, organization, and history. They don't provide much by way of nourishment for the work of the speculative political scientist. But they do provide essential data about how at least one agency of the American state understands that state and shows it to those who would like to embrace it. Creeds and catechisms do this for the church and its doctrine, and are important in something like the same way.

That's not the only reason theologians need to know and use creeds and catechisms. These things are also authoritative to a greater or lesser degree—they bear some magisterial weight and have a status, therefore, that exceeds that of a local and contingent presentation of Catholic doctrine. They are, in different ways and to different degrees, the teaching church's authoritative self-presentation. This is obvious enough in the case of the creeds recited liturgically; those are the collective voice of the church confessing the understanding it has received from the LORD of that same LORD. It's not so obvious in the case of the catechisms. That is in part because the majority of the church's catechisms have been, as many still are, of local origin and local use only. The various Baltimore Catechisms produced in the United States from the mid-nineteenth century onwards were like this; they were widely used for eighty or ninety years, but have now largely passed from use, and were only ever relevant to and used by the church in one locale. But it's also because even the catechisms composed for universal use—the *Roman Catechism* (1566), and the *Catechism of the Catholic Church* (1992)—are best thought of as having no authority independent of or additional to the sources upon which they are based. Nevertheless, because those sources are themselves often of considerable weight (scripture, conciliar texts, papal bulls, and encyclicals), and because the universal catechisms are themselves rooted in conciliar decrees or come with papal authorization, they are themselves sources of considerable authority for the theologian.

Catechisms are useful for Catholic theologians—handy, in the literal sense that they can easily be carried about and that it's easy to look things up in them. They provide a clear view, too, of what the church thought it essential to codify for pedagogical purposes at a particular time, and of the schema used to codify it. The principal universal catechisms should be, in their Latin typical editions and whatever vernacular is of local importance, an often-consulted part of the working library of every theologian. They're as important, and as limited, as dictionaries and manuals of style; which is at least to say that no theological enterprise should be undertaken or prosecuted without consulting them.

---

§22 CANON LAW

The Catholic church, like all long-lived, large-scale communities, has its life ordered in part by codified law. This body of law has come to be called "canon law" (*ius canonicus*) by the church, where "canon" bears the meaning of "authoritative list." A compilation of laws governing ecclesial life is therefore a *codex*, or "code"—in the sense of book or bound volume, and in the sense of systematically-ordered collection—of canon law(s), which in Latin is *codex iuris canonici*. This is the title the church has used for its universal book of laws (there are also collections with local relevance only) since 1917, when Benedict XV promulgated a work with this title. That code remained in force until 1983, when John Paul II, in the Apostolic Constitution *Sacrae disciplinae leges* (Laws of Sacred Discipline), promulgated a revised Code, which remains in force today. Before the twentieth century, there were many local codes, as well as, for the universal church by the fifteenth century, an unwieldy collection of canons with a structure so complex as to make it nearly unusable. This was called the *Corpus iuris canonici* (Body of Canon Law).

Both the 1917 Code and its 1983 successor ought often to be in Catholic theologians' hands. Sometimes, for particular theological questions, it's necessary also to consult earlier collections, but theologians are neither canonists (that is, their task is not to provide reliable or binding interpretations of particular laws) nor historians of canon law (for which specialized skills are necessary), and they do not need to try to become either. Consultation with those who do possess such skill will often be necessary, just as is the case for nonexpert users of secular law codes. In the case of the 1917 and 1983 codes, theologians should consult the Latin versions principally; these are the only authoritative texts, and in the case of law even more than in theology, the Latin language carries a weight of precision and a wealth of suggestion definitively absent from vernacular versions. Those have their uses, however, and a convenient facing-page Latin-English edition of the 1983 code can be had from the Canon Law Society of America. Law, in the sense of codified legislation, is surd until applied; and application by judicial bodies—the Roman Rota, local tribunals and episcopal courts, and so on—requires and provokes commentary on the code. For the English-speaking world a good entry-point into this is the commentary published by the Canon Law Society of America. This, too, should be in theologians' libraries, even though a good portion of the material in it is of only indirect relevance to theological work.

Law is not theology. It prescribes norms that order the life of a community, sanctions to be applied when those norms are contravened, procedures to be used when applying the norms and effecting the sanctions, and other matters of that sort. Why, then, do theologians need to know and consult these legal codes? Because the community whose life the canons of the codes norm is the church, those made members of Christ's body by baptism. The norms that order the life of that community are of profound, direct, and sometimes explicit theological relevance. They have something to say, that is, about the LORD, refracted through the necessity of providing norms for the life of the people most intimate with the LORD. A high proportion of the 1,752 canons in the 1983 Code treats directly how it is that the members of Christ's body ought to live together—what their rights and duties are; what states of life are possible for them; what the sacraments are that sanctify them and how they ought be administered; what the teaching office of the church is and how it ought be manifested, understood, and otherwise responded to; how, and under what conditions, it is possible for the church corporately or its members severally to own property; what are the relations between the prescriptions, proscriptions, and norms of the Code and those of the civil codes that bear locally upon the baptized—and so on. Theologians need to know this material, or at least know how to find their way around in it and to consult those skilled in its interpretation; at the very least, what's said in the *Code* is often of relevance to the formulation and analysis of theological questions, and the theological payoff is often much richer than that.

The codes will appear differently to and be used differently by the faith-filled and baptized Catholic theologian than to and by those doing Catholic theology from outside the church. The former understand themselves to be bound by the canons of the codes they study and make theological use of; they understand those canons, too, to be Spirit-guided and really to show what the LORD wants for the community established by the death, resurrection, and ascension of Jesus of Nazareth. The latter understand it, rather, as setting forth the norms the community that so understands itself takes to govern its life with the LORD here in the devastation. For both groups, the theological yield of studying the codes is great, and the importance for the theological enterprise of such study is non-negotiable.

§23 LITURGY

The most distinctive and characteristic activity of the church is worship of the triune LORD in the name of Jesus. The extent to which a community does this is the extent to which it is the church; the extent to which it fails to do this, whether by doing it imperfectly or by not doing it at all, is the extent to which it is not the church. Everything else that members of Christ's body (the baptized) do is also done by others, more or less; but not this, not worship of the triune LORD in the name of Jesus; that's what Christians, and only they, do. The church is evident in its purest and most concentrated form exactly when its members, who are Christ's members, are gathered in worship. In formally similar ways, the university is evident in its purest and most concentratedly characteristic form when its members are seeking and communicating cognitive intimacy with an object of study; and the Chicago White Sox is most fully itself when its members are playing baseball. Everything else that the church (or the university or the White Sox) does is ancillary—essential, perhaps, but in the service of something more distinctive, more characteristic, more proper to its nature and purpose.

Because worship of the triune LORD in the name of Jesus is what the church does when most fully itself, the ecclesial archive contains many liturgical books. These contain, typically, the full texts (verbal and/or musical) to be said or sung aloud by any or all of the participants in a liturgy; verbal rubrics, not themselves vocalized, to specify the proper use of the liturgical texts ("the people say ..."), as well as other matters such as the appropriate bodily posture of the participants ("the congregation kneels," "the priest anoints with chrism"), which are not themselves said; and, sometimes, prefatory and explanatory material of various kinds.

The typical editions—the authoritative ones, from which all other versions are made—are, for the Roman Rite (there are other rites within the church), in Latin and are prepared and authorized in Rome, typically under the aegis of the *Congregatio de Cultu Divino et Disciplina Sacramentorum* (Congregation for Divine Worship and the Discipline of the Sacraments). Vernacular editions are then prepared and authorized by local episcopal synods, ordinarily with approval from Rome as well. These procedures are designed to ensure uniformity. The rites of the church are meant to be in essentials the same wherever and whenever celebrated because their form is understood to be itself an element of the deposit of faith. Uniformity of worship in practice extends (usually: there are always exceptions on the ground) as far as the structure and content of any particular rite, but the rubrics always leave room for local variation within the given structure, much as stage directions always, and necessarily, leave room for variation in performance even when the text remains invariant.

The central rites of the church, those performed most frequently and given the most liturgical attention (the liturgical books devoted to them are the longest and most internally complex) are, first, the fully sacramental. Within these, the *ordo missae* (order of the mass) is central; the others—baptism, confirmation, ordination, penance, marriage, anointing of the sick—circle the mass like planets the sun. There are liturgical books for all these rites, available both separately and bound together in various combinations. They undergo occasional revision: the latest revision of the third edition of the *Missale Romanum* (Roman Missal), for example, was promulgated in 2008. Vernacular editions are also regularly (but not frequently) revised, sometimes because of pressures internal to a particular language-area, and always (in theory; in practice often belatedly) in response to revisions in the Latin typical edition. The most recent revision to the order of the mass for the English-speaking world, for example, came into effect in 2011.

Second, there are rites to be performed daily, ideally at set times, as a means of ordering and sanctifying the daily cycle of time. The official name of these rites now, since the Second Vatican Council, is *Liturgia Horarum*, the liturgy of the hours. They are important for the church's liturgical life, in one sense as important as the fully sacramental rites; but they are considerably less widely used than those. The liturgy of the hours consist of prayers and scriptural readings indexed to the time of day and the (liturgical) season of the year; their celebration does not require the presence of a priest or deacon; like the sacramental liturgical books, those that contain the liturgy of the hours provide all the texts to be sung or said, together with rubrics specifying their use, prefatory historical and explanatory material, and ancillary helps—tables of liturgical days and suchlike. These rites have their origin in the monastery, where they still mostly flourish; their regular use is also prescribed for every priest. There are many other occasional rites: for the blessing of occasions and objects, for the performance of funerals, for exorcisms, for the consecration of space, for public lament, and so on. All these have their authoritative liturgical forms, as well, though some of them are performed only locally and therefore have no universal form or use.

A large portion of the archive consists of liturgical books, and because of the centrality of liturgical action to the life of the church, these are understood by the curators of the archive to be central to it—as important in their own way as scripture, conciliar texts, canon law, and the deliverances of the ordinary and universal magisterium. These books are, however, less explicitly theological—less explicitly about the LORD—than, for example, scripture or the conciliar texts. Their rubrics regulate performance; and their content—the texts spoken or sung—are mostly in the mode of direct address to the LORD rather than in that of thought about the LORD. What's said in the liturgy, and therefore what's found in the liturgical books, is mostly the language of love and lament rather than the language of ratiocination about the LORD. Most of the content of the liturgical books, too, comes from other parts of the archive: they contain the creeds because these are recited in unison and they contain large parts of scripture. And so it's reasonable to ask: What use have these books for theologians? What can be done with them theologically?

Much can be done. Knowledge and use of these books is essential for Catholic theologians, whether or not they are lovers and worshipers of the LORD, because the books show, in detail and explicitly, at least the following: how Catholic Christians address and respond to the LORD when they are gathered for worship; which aspects of human life are understood to be in special need of regulation and ordering toward the LORD; which modes of speech and action are thought appropriate—and, therefore, which inappropriate—for address to the LORD; how Catholic Christians dispose, order, and relate themselves to the past, especially the past of the people of Israel and the past of the church; how time is ordered, represented, and inhabited, whether at the level of the day, the week, or the year; and so on. All this is data for the theologian. It provides matter for theological thought, even though what's in the liturgical books—texts and rubrics—is not itself theological because it is not aimed principally at cognitive intimacy with the LORD and therefore doesn't distance itself from the LORD in order to look at and describe the LORD as theology proper does and must do. The liturgical books do, sometimes, contain theology. They reproduce the texts of the creeds, for example, which have some theology in them. But the liturgical books use the theology they contain to nurture worshipers' affective and spiritual intimacy with the LORD; and since what theologians are after is cognitive intimacy, which is a different matter, they must reframe and redirect what they find in the liturgical books for their own purposes.

For example, the daily cycle of the liturgy of the hours specifies prayers and scriptural readings for particular hours of the day. *Laudes Matutinae* (morning prayer) is said, obviously, in the morning, ideally upon waking; *Completorium* (compline) is said before sleeping; and other prayers belong to other hours—midday, evening, and so on. Neither the rubrics for the prayers belonging to these hours, nor the scriptural texts and prayer texts themselves, have much to say about why the day is ordered as it is; neither, with only few and insignificant exceptions, do they have anything to say about why this or that prayer belongs to this or that time of day. The material is simply there, given; its rubrics, too, are close to the ground, saying only enough—like stage directions and the texts of the plays they direct—to permit, in practice, easy and (relatively) uniform use of the texts by those who wish to pray them. Theologians looking at this material, whether they do it by studying the liturgical books, by looking at what people who use them do, or (ideally) both, ought to have questions about it not explicitly answered by it. They might ask about the understanding of time signaled (suggested, implied, even entailed) by the fact that the twenty-four-hour daily cycle is ordered in this way. They might ask, more particularly, about the significance of repetition for the inculcation of an understanding of time on the part of those who regularly pray the liturgy of the hours, whether in whole or in part. There are suggestive signals within the parts of the prayer-cycle itself about the relation that each part bears to every other, and about the meaning of the fact that there is an endlessly repeated cycle. All this is fodder for ruminant theologians. They might begin to speculate about the relation between time ordered cyclically (as by the liturgy of the hours) and time ordered linearly (as by a watch or a calendar). Out of that speculation might come a sketch of a Christian-theological understanding of the temporal order. Such a sketch would be quite out of place as an element of any liturgical book; those books, rather, are its stimulus, the matter to which it responds.

Working theologians ought have easily to hand the essential liturgical books and ought to often consult them. These may be divided into two kinds. First, there are those that provide the texts and rubrics for the repeated and usually cyclical rites, participation in which is, in some fashion and with varying frequency, incumbent upon all Catholic Christians. Paradigmatic here is the missal, with its lectionary, the books containing the liturgy of the hours, and the order for the celebration of the rite of penance or reconciliation. Second, there are the rites, with their corresponding books, which are typically, or at least ideally, celebrated only once in the life of a Christian (baptism, confirmation, viaticum, marriage, ordination). Some of these (baptism, confirmation, viaticum) are incumbent upon, or at least proper to, all Christians; others (marriage, ordination) are the means of entry into states of life possible and appropriate for some, but not required for all. The liturgical books for all these rites have their authoritative Latin typical editions, produced and curated by the Congregation for Divine Worship, and these ought to be the point of first refuge for the working theologian. There are also, for most nations and language communities, vernacular versions of these books approved for use by the local episcopal synod, and these, too, ought be to hand.

Worship is done—performed, undertaken—as well as written about in books. Baptized and believing Catholic theologians are likely to be worshipers, too. That's not because they're theologians; it's because they're baptized. It belongs to the vocation of the baptized to worship. It doesn't belong to the vocation of the theologian to do so. Nonetheless, those theologians, baptized or not, faithful or not, who do worship are likely to find their theological thinking invigorated and enriched in various ways by worship in something like the same way that those whose only acquaintance with Shakespeare is on the page find their appreciation and understanding of the texts deepened by seeing them performed—and still more by performing in them. Active liturgical participation is more difficult and more complex for the unbaptized, and therefore generally less available to them as a source and stimulus for theological thought and writing. This is a disadvantage, no doubt. But it is not simply that. As with love's knowledge, the theological stimulus and formation provided by participation in the liturgy comes with its own lacks. Principal among these is that theologians who are worshipers will never know what it is like to study and make theological use of the church's liturgical books without participating in what they regulate. Theologians who don't worship know this and can, as a result, see things hidden to worshipers, rather as readers of Shakespeare can see things hidden from those who have only seen Shakespeare performed, or those who can no longer separate their Shakespearean reading from their formation by performance.

§24 THE NONTEXTUAL ARCHIVE

Christians don't only, or mostly, produce texts, and the Christian archive isn't, therefore, mostly or only textual. It contains a vast quantity of nontextual material objects, including at least: buildings, paintings, statuary, musical scores, body parts used as relics, graveyards, and liturgical implements. Some of these are in active use; others are, in one way or another, preserved as museum pieces; and others—the vast majority—exist as ruins or remains. I grew up in a country—England—whose countryside is dotted with the spectacular and mournful skeletal remains of abbeys and monasteries devastated by the Reformation. Much of the Christian archive, textual and otherwise, has perished in still more radical ways than this, leaving, effectively, nothing behind. Only a small portion remains of the churches built by Christians, the paintings and statues made by them, the music composed by them, the chalices burnished by them, the hair and bones and teeth and organs of their dead. The rest has gone.

It's not easy, and perhaps not possible, to provide criteria that neatly separates what belongs to the Christian archive from what doesn't. Bright lines here, as in most cases, aren't available. A good rule of thumb is that the more intimate an artifact is with the worship of the triune LORD who is the god of Israel—this is the distinctively Christian activity, the thing that Christians do which is most characteristic of them and which others don't do, at least not under that description—the stronger the case for saying that it belongs to the nontextual Christian archive. Chalices, patens, altars, church buildings—those are clear cases. Paintings of scriptural scenes commissioned and hung privately are less clear cases; they may never have been intended or used for anything to do with worship.

The nontextual archive isn't directly theological. It doesn't, that's to say, deploy the methods proper to theology, and isn't aimed principally at that cognitive intimacy with the LORD which is theology's primary purpose. Much of it consists of things needed for and used in worship—buildings, liturgical implements, much statuary and carving and painting, and so on; and some is intended to shape and arouse the user's affections and passions by turning them toward the LORD, or to show what it is like to live as a human creature in a world made by the LORD and devastated by sin—this applies to much art and music.

These artifacts, though not themselves theological, can be of use to theologians. They typically suggest how the Christians who made and used them understood and related to the LORD in whose service they were deployed. Caravaggio's painting *Madonna dei Palafrenieri*, for instance, an early seventeenth-century (probably 1605–6) painting commissioned to decorate an altar in St. Peter's at Rome and now hung in the Galleria Borghese, arguably belongs to the Christian archive. This is true even though it was only briefly hung where worship was performed, and even though Caravaggio's motives in painting it and Scipio Borghese's in (eventually) buying it probably had little to do with Christian piety. The painting depicts a Christian scene: Anne, Mary's mother and Jesus's grandmother, shown as an old woman, perhaps in her seventies, stands right, looking at the ground where a snake lashes violently, its head trapped under Mary's left foot. Mary, in turn, is shown as a beautiful woman in her twenties or thirties, dressed in a low-cut red and green gown and with her feet (or at least the visible one) bare, bending slightly at the waist with her gaze fixed on the snake, holding the naked boy-child Jesus with his foot on top of hers. The snake's head is trapped by both feet, hers and

Jesus's, but with Mary's the only one in direct contact with it. Jesus is shown as a boy of about seven, naked, with a head of curly red-gold hair, uncircumcised, and with the straight lines of his extended left leg and his penis aimed directly at the snake's head. The background is dark; light coming from the left illuminates the three human faces, Mary's neck and breasts, and, especially, Jesus's naked flesh. The three figures are intimately and directly present to the viewer.

This is all theologically suggestive. It raises questions about the relation between what Mary does and what Jesus does in trapping the snake. Is she showing him how to do this, or is she being instructed by him in how to do it? Or both? What significance has the fact that it's her foot directly on the snake's head rather than his? How should the viewer think about the aged but intent figure of Anne? Is it significant, and if so how, that Jesus is shown uncircumcised? Mariology, Christology, soteriology, the relations between divine and human agency, the nature of evil's agency (that snake's contortions)—all these are in play in the painting. This painting has no magisterial significance; we, its twenty-first-century viewers, know next to nothing about Caravaggio's intentions in painting it or those of its commissioners in commissioning it; we do, or can, know something about its controversial reception and subsequent history, and something is no doubt known (though not to me) about sixteenth- and seventeenth-century Italian conventions concerning depictions of Anne, Mary, and Jesus. None of this determines the theological use of the painting, though all of it may be deployed by theologians who want to use artifacts like this as aids to and prompts for theological thinking—which is exactly the principal use, for Catholic theologians, of the nontextual archive. Looking at Caravaggio, listening to Messiaen, or Bach, or Pärt, or Gubaidulina, or Saarahio, gazing at altarpieces and graveyards and relics—these are devices for stimulating theological thought, thought about the LORD, that is; they are powerful devices and should be used often by theologians. They are fecund in generating properly theological questions and patterns of thought, even if they aren't themselves fully theological.

Nevertheless, the textual archive remains the principal resource for theologians. Theology is, first and last, a matter of words, distinctions, arguments, and entailments. It requires fluency in the grammar of Christian-theological talk, and the tool of most importance for developing such fluency is exactly those parts of the archive that exemplify fluency, which is to say the textual archive. The nontextual elements of the archive are useful, suggestive, perhaps even essential as stimuli; but they remain, for theologians, ancillary. Quite the reverse is the case for faithful and practicing Christians. That is another way of saying that the practice of theology is an insignificant element of the Christian life.

---

§25 SKILLS

The textual archive contains what theologians need to know. Acquaintance with its scope and content is therefore essential for them. Deep and wide reading in it may, and sometimes does, provide the skills necessary for theological work; but those skills are not identical with knowledge of the archive's content, no matter how extensive and thorough it is. Particular skills are needed in order to make theological work with the archive possible. First among them is fluency in Christian-theological discourse, which means knowing and being able to use its lexicon and syntax. Second, the capacity to recognize and generate theological questions, which is to say questions about the LORD; identifying and asking questions of that sort is among the principal generators of theological discourse. Third, the skill of making perspicuous and precise distinctions in the service of exploring theological questions by suggesting trajectories of thought about them, and even, sometimes, answers to them. Fourth, argumentative ability, which is to say a taste and capacity for offering arguments, *pro* and *contra*, about theological positions; thought doesn't get far without that capacity, because arguments are what place it under pressure, and pressure is what, more than anything else, gives shape to thought. These four skills are generically intellectual: they belong to any and every intellectual enterprise, and thus also to the theological one. Theologians need them as much as—perhaps more than—other intellectuals; it's one of the characteristic errors of would-be theologians to underestimate, and even to devalue, the properly intellectual demands of the endeavor they're undertaking. Faith, devotion, passion, orthodoxy—these are all good things, but they have little to do with intellectual skill (they certainly don't supply it), and that skill is essential for theologians.

Underlying and informing these generically intellectual skills are some specific to the theological enterprise. First, there is discovery: because there is settled doctrine on some matters, theologians, if they are to do (for example) Catholic theology, must know how to discover whether there is settled doctrine about the topics that concern them, and, if there is, what it is. Failure to do this, whether because it's thought irrelevant to the theological enterprise or because it's done badly, entails the failure of the discourse that results to be Catholic theology. It may be theology as discourse about the LORD; but it won't be Catholic theology because the grammar of that discourse includes the idea that there is settled, authoritative doctrine about at least some theological topics, and that what theologians say and think in their speculative moods must identify and be responsive to it.

No doctrinal position, no matter how well established and how long the history of its magisterial deployment, is beyond further interpretive questioning. It is incumbent upon theologians to interpret the doctrine they discover: to offer, that is, a more-or-less speculative position as to what it should be taken to mean. Discovery and interpretation lead to speculation, which is the activity of offering and arguing for ways of thinking about—and sometimes answers to—theological questions which the tradition has not authoritatively answered, and perhaps not even recognized. The speculative performance requires and deploys all the generic skills of the intellectual: fluency, questioning, distinction-making, and argument; its aim is to offer to whatever audience theologians take themselves to be addressing (this will be different for faith-filled Catholics than for those doing Catholic theology from without) a position to be entertained on some theological question. Good speculation results in more of the same; it is conversational and provocative; it expects response, riposte, disagreement, development. Bad speculation fails to provoke; it falls deadborn from the press, unread from the blog, untweeted on Twitter, unliked on Facebook.

The (four) generically intellectual skills and the (three) specifically theological ones aren't typically, or perhaps ever, developed in plodding sequential order. Theologians don't first become fluent, then questioning, and at last speculative. Each skill requires the others, and better images than the ladder for understanding their relations are those of the feedback loop and the multi-directional and multi-linked helix. Theologians move constantly back and forth among the various skills: as they question, they use discovery to see what they need to engage the question; discovering provokes distinction-making, which moves to speculation, and then back to argument. The skills form a fabric whose threads aren't easy to unpick. The value of distinguishing the various skills one from another is heuristic only, but may nevertheless be great. Such distinctions can, for example, help would-be theologians to see what they're good at and what they're not good at, and to identify aspects of the theological enterprise they may be disposed to shortchange. Those discernments are great goods.

Treating know-how (the development of theological skill) separately from knowing-that (acquaintance with the archive's scope and content) is helpful in another way as well. It underscores the fact that learning, understood as acquaintance with the archive, is, while necessary for theologians, radically insufficient for the practice of theology. Historians and exegetes, the virtuosos of the archive and (too often) its self-appointed guardians, usually aren't much good at or much interested in theology. What marks theologians is speculative interest and intellectual skill; they aren't necessarily adequate or reliable guides to the archive. That doesn't mean they can prescind from it: it belongs to the grammar of Catholic theological discourse to account for and respond to it. But it does mean that such accounting and response isn't their primary concern, and that they may often need correction and guidance from those whose primary concern it is. In reading theology, the neophyte theologian should seek those with highly developed intellectual and speculative skills and pay less attention to those whose primary concerns are retrieval and exegesis. Again, there's no bright line; everyone does some of both. But the specific gifts and aims of theological discourse ought always be kept in mind by those who wish to undertake it, and those gifts and aims are, principally, grammatical, intellectual, and speculative.

§26 ABSTRACTION AND IMAGINATION

Underlying and interwoven with the acquisition of know-how and knowing-that on the part of theologians ought be the development of intellectual imagination. That kind of imagination combines seeing the bones of a theological position—its deep structure, what gives it the shape it has—with seeing how that structure might be added to, extended, adjusted, or, in extreme cases, gutted to the studs and reconstructed, as one might with an old house; or disassembled and put back together differently, as one does when rearranging furniture in a room. Seeing through flesh to bone doesn't come naturally to anyone, and easily only to a few. It's essentially a skill in radical abstraction: reduction, that is, of a theological position elucidated in the prose of some natural language with all its lovely freight of semantic and historical particularity to something as close as possible to the formulae of the propositional calculus, tokens with logical properties only, their particularities burned off in something like the way that an influx of capital burns off the nuance from a local culture. Abstraction is a consuming fire, just like capital; what it consumes, or attempts to, is ambiguity and local particularity; what it seeks is precision and universality. The world of abstraction isn't habitable for long, but it's a world that theologians need to learn to enter and exit at will. Once the bones of a position are clear to a theologian's gaze, it becomes easier to see what might be done with them; when the knee joint is enfleshed, it's hard to see how it works, how it might be fixed if something isn't working as it ought, and how its design might be improved; but when it's studied skeletally or as an x-ray image, those things are easier to see. Similarly, abstraction, the more radical the better, is important as a precursor to imagining adjustment, improvement, reconstruction, and extension.

Abstraction by itself doesn't always yield imaginative vision. The anatomist isn't necessarily a good reconstructive surgeon or a good designer of prostheses. The imaginative capacity for such things as those is in part a gift, like those for musical composition or improvisation, and in part a skill to be nurtured by experiment. Theologians, like neophyte composers of poets or painters, need to look at examples of how it's done—of how a theological position is analyzed, taken apart, reconstructed, extended, and (when things go well) improved—and to do so without caring, for the purposes of the exercise, whether the upshot is acceptable or admirable. This distance is necessary in order that the skill be developed exactly as a skill—a *techne* that can be practiced independently of concern about its outcome. Further, the exercise needs to be done repeatedly and mechanically so that it becomes habitual, something the habituated mind reaches out to and performs as pianists' fingers do the keyboard. For example, close attention to the structure of Augustine's *De trinitate* (The Trinity) or *De civitate dei* (City of God) shows the bones of those works: how they're ordered and, often, why they're ordered as they are and not in some other way. Clear sight of these bones is revelatory of a series of conceptual decisions, and gaining such sight helps neophytes (and advanced students—all of us always have more to learn about this) to see how theological work is done, and thus begin to see how they might do it themselves.

§27 FLUENCY

Theologians need fluency in the grammar of Christian theology. It's the first and essential tool of their trade. Fluency is unthinking ease. It's the ability to do something without accompanying effort, strain, or difficulty. I can speak English in that way, place one foot before the other as I walk down the street, make meaning from a printed page of English prose, kiss my beloved, drive my car, and deploy the grammar of orthodox Catholic theology. By contrast, I largely lack fluency's ease at manipulating three-dimensional objects in space, at knowing which point of the compass I'm headed toward, at reading poetry in German, and many other things. And then there are performances I've seen people give—quickly finding cube roots in the head, conducting a symphony orchestra in a performance of Shostakovich's Seventh Symphony, singing Papagena in the *Magic Flute*, extemporizing sonnets, hitting home runs—at which I not only lack fluency but cannot in the least imagine what it would be like to have it. Formally, however, fluency is always arrived at in the same way: by deep habituation over time. The more often you do something, the better, ordinarily, you get at doing it. Parents see this in their children: the first steps are uncertain and unsteady, hard to repeat and frequently failing; the first words are hard to recognize, and tend to be ejaculations rather than clauses or sentences (syntax comes hard). But soon enough, with repetition, the staggering and incomprehensible twelve-month-old is, by the age of three, running gracefully and speaking in well-formed sentences without apparent effort. Fluency has been reached, mostly by habituation. What theologians need is fluency in theological grammar, and that is to be had in just the same way as infants learn to speak and walk: by imitation and by catechesis.

Fluency is a matter of degree. It's not that you either have it or don't have it; rather, you have more or less of it and you never have it completely. In that, it's like beauty or height or virtue. These are spectrum-concepts without a maximum though with a minimum, which is complete lack. I completely lack fluency in Xhosa; I have very little of it in Japanese; a little more in French, and a great deal in English. In this, fluency is like all habit-produced skills: such skills wax and wane according to the extent to which they're practiced. Although it's common to ask whether someone speaks French, and to expect the answer "yes" or "no," this is a shorthand for something much more complicated. No one simply speaks French; rather, everyone who speaks any at all speaks a kind of French suitable for some purposes but not for all. The mandarin French of a member of the Académie Française may not permit easy comprehension or communication in the banlieues (or in Quebec). When I first visited the Bronx in 1979, even though I was a native speaker of English in its British variety, I could scarcely make myself understood and could understand almost nothing of what was said to me. I learned, and increased my fluency for that purpose, while (no doubt) reducing it for others. That's the way skills work. Aspiring theologians seek, therefore, to increase their fluency in Christian theological grammar; they do not seek fluency *simpliciter* because there's no such thing.

Grammatical fluency, the kind theologians need, comprises fluency in lexicon and syntax. Every discourse has a grammar with these two elements, and the discourse that is Christian theology is no exception. The two—lexicon and syntax—are separable for analytical purposes: the lexicon of a discourse is its preferred or technical vocabulary, the words (lexical items) around which accumulate treasure-houses of meaning via repeated use, commentary, argument, and so on; that discourse's syntax is the body of rules that govern how the lexical items that constitute the discourse's preferred vocabulary may properly be related one to another. These rules are rarely formulated explicitly, and when that is done it's in response to challenge or pressure, typically in the form of a dispute about whether a sentence that combines lexical items in a particular way is well formed. Explicit or not, however, syntactical rules are always operative; no discourse exists or can be maintained without broad agreement among its users as to what they are—agreement that doesn't preclude but, rather, permits intense disagreement about particular cases. Lexical and syntactical skill are therefore separable for purposes of discussion and analysis. But acquisition of one skill always involves some acquisition of the other; understanding a lexicon (itself always a matter of spectrum rather than toggle) always involves (some) understanding of how that lexicon is deployed in sentences; and understanding syntax—subject/verb agreement, say, or appropriate placement of an adjective in relation to the noun it modifies (in English)—never floats entirely free of lexical skill.

Catholic Christianity's preferred theological lexicon—its lexicon for speaking and writing about the triune LORD—includes: god, LORD, Jesus, Christ, Father, Son, Spirit, world, creature, church, sacrament, grace, sin, heaven, hell, salvation, damnation, worship, scripture, prayer, angel, demon, faith, incarnation, inspiration, election, covenant, eschatology, salvation. Anyone who could, without consulting any books and at the drop of a hat, give a one-thousand-word disquisition on each of these words, including comment on etymology, use, semantic content, and disputes concerning it, would be fairly fluent in the lexicon of Christian theology. Any such disquisition would necessarily go beyond the merely lexical; it would include comment on syntactical matters, such as whether it's permissible in Christian-theological discourse to call the Son a creature (it is not), or whether it ought be said that every creature is capable of salvation (a matter of dispute, but the correct speculative answer is yes), or whether the utterance that faith is indefectible is well-formed (a difficult question, hinging on the definition of "faith"; the best speculative answer, once the ground is appropriately cleared, is yes). The degree of one's fluency in Christian theological discourse can be measured in significant part by capacity to do this sort of thing.

Ordinarily, fluencies are multiple and non-competitive. Being relatively fluent in the discourse of baseball doesn't militate against fluency in the discourse of music-criticism or botany; and each of those fluencies is parasitic upon fluency in English or some other natural language because it is learned and performed in one of them. Most human creatures are non-competitively fluent in many discourses in this way. But the discourse that is Catholic theology is in one very important way not like this. It can stand alongside other fluencies; nothing about being a good—fluent—theologian prevents being a fluent lepidopterist or automechanic. But theological discourse is related to these other discourses as master to slave, in the sense that skill in theological discourse carries with it the judgment that all other discourses are subordinate to it, at least in the sense that it provides an interpretive frame for them which they cannot provide for it or for themselves. That's not to say that fluency in theological discourse ordinarily provides the ability to specify in detail how other discourses should proceed, or to assess particular instances of those discourses: becoming a good theologian, even a paradigmatic one, a *doctor ecclesiae*, won't provide any help in assessing a proffered proof of Fermat's Last Theorem (that's a matter for mathematicians), or in deciding the degree of autonomy that the U.S. Constitution provides to state courts (that's a matter for jurists).

But it is to say that theological discourse can, according to its own self-understanding (that is, it belongs to theology to say this about itself), provide an account of all other discourses of a scope, precision, and unsurpassability which they cannot provide even about themselves, and much less about discourses other than themselves. Theologians can explain what mathematics (or sociology or economics or philosophy) is in a manner unavailable to mathematicians, and in doing so can formulate truths about mathematics and the rest unavailable to mathematicians. Theological discourse is imperial in this way; coming to see that fact about it—that feature of it—is an aspect of fluency in Christian (or at least in Catholic) theological discourse. Bonaventure's maxim, *omnes cognitiones famulantur theologiae* (every kind of cognition is theology's slave), from his treatise *De reductione artium ad theologiam* (The Reduction of the Arts to Theology), can serve as a mnemonic for this view. It means at least that theological discourse provides an unframeable frame, a discourse that cannot be accounted for by any other, and which, therefore, participates as a creature can (all discourse is by necessity creaturely) in a feature of the LORD, which is that of being *id quo maius non cogitari possit* (that than which nothing greater can be conceived), as Anselm puts it in the *Proslogion*. Modes of knowing (*cognitiones*) serve theology—theology transcends and accounts for them—in a way formally analogous to the way in which the LORD transcends human knowing (*cognitio*). To become fluent in theological discourse involves, though isn't exhausted by, coming to know and be able to say these things about the LORD and about discourse that concerns itself with the LORD. Theological fluency configures those who have it, therefore, in a very particular way of understanding, relating to, and accounting for all the non-theological discourses.

Theological fluency, like all skills, is received, deepened, and made flexible by catechesis. To learn how to speak and write as theologians do, what's needed, first and last, is to spend time with those already fluent in that kind of talk, to attend closely to what they say and how they say it, to imitate their discourse, be challenged and corrected by it, and thus to become a performer. Neophyte theologians, this is to say, must serve an apprenticeship which largely consists in listening to (reading) other theologians. This theological listening (reading) ought be partly passive and partly active. Passively, osmotically, ambient theological discourse can be soaked up simply by being in its company. If your companions speak and write theology, and you spend time with them, you, perforce and without (much) effort, learn to speak and write it, too, in much the same way that you learned to speak your mother tongue. Theological company isn't easy to come by, however; you're unlikely to find it serendipitously, and so you'll need to seek it out. That isn't difficult to do in the sphere of the text. There's lots of theological writing, and it's mostly easy enough to find. A large proportion of the writings of the *doctores ecclesiae*, for instance, is available in many languages on the web; a judicious use of Amazon will provide you with a vast theological library, Catholic, Protestant, and Orthodox, in the language of your choice, should you be able to afford it; any large library system, public or private, will have a significant theological collection; and there is now to hand at the touch of a button or the click of a cursor a massy mountain range of more obscure theological texts, postmodern, modern, and premodern, the vagaries of copyright law permitting, by way of resources such as Google Scholar. The neophyte in search of fluency should make use of all this: aspiring theologians should have it as a rule of life always to have some theological reading under way. Making such reading a central (but never the only) part of a reading life will, inevitably and insensibly, produce some degree of theological fluency.

But isn't it difficult for theologians with little or no fluency to decide what they ought to read? The archive is vast; selecting from it seems to require knowledge neophytes must, by definition, lack. That's true, but there's a rule of thumb that provides a partial but surprisingly powerful answer to it. Catholics in search of theological reading might choose one of the *doctores ecclesiae* (their names and some information about them and their principal works are provided at the end of this book), begin to collect a library of work by them (and perhaps also about them, though that should be a secondary consideration), and to read them, repeatedly and for the long haul. Some among them (Augustine, Aquinas) have a very extensive corpus, large enough to serve as a lifetime's companion; this is less true of others (Teresa of Avila, Cyril of Jerusalem, Thérèse of Lisieux), but because theological texts—especially those by the *doctores*—are rarely exhausted by a single reading, even they can serve as companions and instructors for much of a reading life. Observing this rule of thumb can provide a theological interlocutor whose modes of thought, preferred vocabulary, particular obsessions, and other idiosyncrasies, form the reader, sometimes insensibly and sometimes with effort and intention, as a theologian. That the chosen interlocutor is a *doctor* means that her or his work has already been judged to be important for the theological work of the church; neophytes therefore don't have to be concerned about the status of the interlocutor they've chosen. Osmotic reading of this sort is a necessary device for increasing fluency. It doesn't require instruction or guidance; it works insensibly on those who do it, just as does anything else done repeatedly over time. No theologian should be without it, and none, even the most fluent, should give it up. It's simply part of the theologian's life repeatedly to read theology.

Osmotic reading isn't enough. Theology is a *techne*, and therefore its literature is often technical in the sense that it doesn't easily yield itself to the amateur, the one who simply reads without guidance in how to read. To read a question of Thomas's *Summa Theologiae* without guidance isn't easy and may often mislead. The same is true, in different ways, for Teresa of Avila's

Interior Castle, or Edith Stein's work on empathy. Even with a reading habit in place or under development, therefore, aspiring theologians must seek guidance that can't be had from texts. They need teachers and peers, living people who can teach them and develop their fluency by face-to-face exchange. This isn't so easy. It requires, usually, finding an institution where professional theologians do their work, and that means a university, where most theology is now done; a seminary (some of which are connected to universities, and some of which are freestanding), where priests are trained; or a religious house where aspirants to some religious order or other are trained and tested and formed. Those are the places where almost all theologians beyond the neophyte stage are to be found; they're also where the largest groups of theologians-in-training are. Those serious about learning theology need, almost without exception, to find such places and undergo apprentice training in them. Only in that way can they be guided in how to read what they ought read, and in the traditions of interpretation and disagreement that belong to the Christian archive, and that often proceed by argument about how best to treat the classic texts of the archive—scriptural, magisterial, legal, liturgical, speculative, and so on.

Fluency cannot be had only by reading. Oral instruction is necessary, and not only for what can be learned from it about how to read the textual archive better. Oral instruction exposes students to aspects of the archive available only orally: all long-lived traditions of inquiry, but most especially those that form schools of thought to which lineage is important—this is very much the case for Catholicism—have such an oral dimension. Generalizations about what it contains and hands on are difficult because of the particularities of the orders and schools—a training in reading the archive received at Benedictine hands is very different from one given by Jesuits; each is different again from those given by

Dominicans or Franciscans, which in turn differ significantly one from another; but all orally transmitted training in fluency includes modeling of and instruction in modes of argument, interpretation, and pedagogy of a depth and thickness unavailable in texts. Some of these engage and treat the written archive; but some are distinctively oral, and operate only or largely in that sphere. Training in methods of speaking and argumentation is often like this. All this is as true of theological formation in the secular academy as it is of formation in seminaries or houses run by religious orders: the doctoral seminar and the dissertation defense, both definitionally oral events, hand on a kind of oral fluency proper to secular academic training.

Fluency is as necessary for extra-ecclesial (pagan, academic, and other) theologians as for ecclesial (faith-filled, Catholic) ones, and since it can only be had by frequent and deep reading in the archive coupled with and deepened by oral instruction from the lips of those more fluent, it must be pursued in the same way by each. That, again, is because theology is a *techne* of the intellect, and for any such skill the methods of attaining it are effectively the same for all. Extra-ecclesial theologians, therefore, perforce use the same sources and the same methods to gain fluency as do ecclesial ones, and there ought be no barriers set in the way of those wishing to do so.

---

§28 MAKING THE INVISIBLE VISIBLE

Those who wish to develop fluency need the company and instruction of those already fluent, whether dead, when the only way they can keep intellectual formative company with us is by way of their literary remains, or living, when they're also sometimes available to us face-to-face, as well as in their texts, if they've composed any. Seekers after fluency need wide, deep, and repeated reading; they also need explicit and face-to-face teaching. These, if the student's gifts and energies are sufficient, yield respectable fluency in Christian theological speech.

But more is both possible and desirable: aspiring theologians need not only to read and not only to be instructed about what they read; they need also to learn to enter and occupy the phenomenological attitude toward what they read. They need, that is, not only to learn the grammar of what they read by osmosis and instruction, but also to learn to look at how the texts they read do what they do—to look closely at what is ordinarily, in the act of reading, looked through without being remarked upon. To do that—to look closely at what's ordinarily transparent and unremarked—exactly is to adopt the phenomenological attitude.

Phenomenologists attend to the structure and order of appearances in unusual ways. When you look a three-dimensional object, for example, it appears to you—shows itself to you—only in part; it's never the case, indeed it can't be the case for creatures equipped sensorily as we are, that a three-dimensional object is seen by us all at once. Ingenious arrangements of mirrors can permit you to see all six sides of a cube at once, but then you're seeing some of those sides indirectly, as a reflected image, and others directly, mediated only by the ordinary mechanisms of vision. This lack isn't a problem; it's not even a lack. You don't feel called upon to walk around to the back of a cube you're looking at to make sure that the sides you can't see are in fact present. You'd be behaving abnormally if you did. What appears to you, what you see, is indeed the cube in its wholeness, in exactly the way that such things are available to creatures like us. But the mode of its appearance, how it does its work upon us, is ordinarily and mostly occluded, or, better, transparent: you look right through it to the thing itself, and you do that exactly so that you may see and interact with the thing itself. Attending closely to how that thing does its work on you would, ordinarily, hamper that work, in something like the same way that attending closely to the shapes made by your beloved's lips as (s)he tells you that (s)he loves you is likely to prevent you, or at least hinder you, from receiving what's said as what it is, a declaration of love.

Adopting the phenomenological attitude isn't easy and doesn't come naturally. While it hides some things, it reveals others that would otherwise remain invisible. The phenomenologist can see, and show, for example, aspects of what it's like to look at a framed painting hanging on a museum's wall that are ordinarily invisible to the looker. By learning what the phenomenologist has to teach about that, lookers at paintings understand something about what they do that would otherwise be hidden from them. This may not, and probably will not, make them better lookers; but it may be of great help if they're trying to learn about the placement of pictures on museum walls, the design of picture frames, or how to think about the difference between twenty-first- and nineteenth-century habits of hanging pictures in museums (the former prefer lots of undecorated space between pictures, the latter very little). For these enterprises, learning what the phenomenological attitude has to teach is useful, and may be essential. If you want to learn how to do something rather than, or as well as, receiving the gift of its having been done for or to you, learning how the thing is done is likely to be useful. Those who go to the theater in order to enjoy a magic show don't need to know how it's done; they don't even need to attend very closely to what appears before their eyes and other senses as the lady is sawn in half or the rabbit pulled from the hat. Were they so to attend, to train themselves in the phenomenological attitude, it's likely that the trick would stop working for them.

Similarly, J. D. Salinger's preferred amateur readers, who share the dedication of *Raise High the Roof Beam, Carpenters, and Seymour, an Introduction* (1963), and are characterized as anyone who "just reads and runs," are exactly those who don't subject what they read to critical analysis; they don't need to know how the novel they're reading does its work in order for it to work on them. They don't need to know about authorial voice, point of view, frame of reference, free indirect speech (that Flaubertian gift), unreliable narrators, and so on. They need to have enough skill in reading whatever language the novel is written in to permit it to do its work on them; but they don't need to know—and they certainly don't need to be able to say—how what it is that appears to them on the page does so. It's possible to read and enjoy Jay McInerny's novel, *Bright Lights, Big City* (1984), say, without realizing, and certainly without being able to say, that the narrative voice is consistently and successfully second-person ("You are not the kind of guy who would be at a place like this at this time of the morning …"). Those who don't realize this aren't necessarily worse readers than those who do; they simply lack an analytical skill that permits technique to show itself. That skill is useful, perhaps, for those who want to write novels, especially those in which there are technical innovations or displays. But for reading? Adopting the phenomenological attitude may be as much of a hindrance as a help.

Devotional readers, who may also be saints or on the way to sainthood, also don't need to know how the theology or hagiography or scripture they read does its work. They read for transformation, in order to increase their love for the LORD, and adopting the phenomenological attitude is ordinarily of no help for that. Theologians, however, those who want not only to read theology for improvement, but also to gain such fluency in theology that they can themselves write it, and who are interested only in cognitive intimacy with the LORD, do need to know what the phenomenological attitude is and how to enter into it. That's because theology is a *techne* of the intellect, and all such require the kind of fluency that involves the phenomenological attitude. This is another reason to underscore the difference between theology and the Christian life, and to emphasize the insignificance of the former for the latter.

§29 *SUMMA THEOLOGIAE* II-II, Q. 19, A. 11

What, more exactly, do aspiring theologians gain from adopting the phenomenological attitude toward what they read, at least some of the time? Observation of the workings of the eleventh article of the nineteenth question of the second half of the second part of Thomas Aquinas's *Summa Theologiae* (Summa of Theology, composed in the 1260s and 1270s)—in brief, *ST* II-II, q. 19, a. 11—gives some idea about this. The general topic of q. 19 is *donum timoris*, the gift of fear, and the specific question of the eleventh article is *utrum [timor] maneat in patria*, whether fear remains in heaven. Readers who read this article without adopting the phenomenological attitude can see clearly that there's a thesis—that there's no fear in heaven, which seems at first blush reasonable, for if heaven contains all and only what is good, and if fear isn't a good, then why would there be fear in heaven? Three supporting arguments for this thesis are given, as amateur readers will also clearly see; and they'll also see that those are followed by an authority, Psalm 19:9, quoted against the opening thesis to the effect that *timor Domini*, fear of the LORD, *permanet in saeculum* (remains forever); and then followed in turn by a *responsio* in which Thomas, speaking in the first person, gives his own opinion on the question, together with supporting arguments. They'll also see that the article concludes with responses, in order, to the three arguments given to buttress the opening thesis. Thomas's view, in brief, is that there are different kinds of *timor*, and that while *timor servilis*, a servile fear that wishes to avoid punishment, is ruled out in heaven because no punishments can occur there, *timor filialis*, filial fear that marks and acknowledges the difference between creature and creator, does remain in heaven because that difference also remains. It is an eternal and structural feature of the relations between the LORD and everything that is not the LORD. Thomas quotes, *inter alia*, Augustine on heavenly fear as holding to a good that can't be lost (*tenens in bono quod amitti non potest*). This is an analogical, or stretched, understanding of fear; affirming it permits Thomas to say that, yes, *timor* does remain in heaven.

That's what the careful and attentive, but also amateur, reader of this article sees. Such readers (and they're good, or good-enough, readers) understand the position Thomas takes, the reasons he gives for taking it, what may be said on the other side of the question (the arguments Thomas gives in support of the thesis he rejects aren't merely decorative; they're strong reasons in support of a position that can reasonably be held), the nature and weight of the authorities quoted, and so on. These are all, more or less, surface features of the text. You don't need the phenomenological attitude to see them.

Readers, whether aspiring theologians or interested observers, who do adopt the phenomenological attitude, see some other things about the text. Their questions are: how does this artifact do its work? How does it appear? Which features of it make it appear and work as it does? Answering these sorts of questions requires attention to features of the text that typically remain invisible to the amateur reader, and even to the sophisticated and attentive reader who is entirely capable of reading, understanding, reprising, and engaging the substance of Thomas's position. It requires, once again, looking at what's ordinarily looked through, and doing so in order to see how what is ordinarily looked at does its work. Rather than looking at the rabbit being pulled from the hat and assessing its appearance and weight, those adopting the phenomenological attitude look at the magician's hands, the pockets of her coat, the movements of her assistants, the configuration of the stage, the sound and lighting effects, and so on—things ordinarily as invisible as the frame of a picture or the wall upon which it's hung to those looking at pictures, but things essential in order that the rabbit should make its entrance, or the picture appear as one before the gaze of its observer. What, in the case of *ST* II-II, q. 19, a. 11, are (some of) these invisibles, and what does it do to readers when they're attended to and become visible?

The first important feature of this kind is the act of distinction-making. The pivot of the article is the point early in the *responsio* where Thomas distinguishes *timor servilis* from *timor filialis*. This conceptual act—a knife-cut, severing one thing from another—makes possible the rebuttal of what otherwise seems an unobjectionable, even an obvious, thesis, which is that there is no fear in heaven, together with the reasons given for it, which are, first, that all fears have an evil or evils as their object, and that since heaven has no evils it likewise has no fears; and, second, that humans in heaven are like the LORD (so says scripture) who is fearless, and so humans in heaven are also fearless; and then, third, that hope is better than fear, but is absent in heaven where all goods are realized (and so there's nothing to hope for), and so fear must also be absent in heaven because it makes no sense that a worse thing could be present where a better thing is absent. These arguments, the *objectiones*, would, were it not for the distinction between the two kinds of fear, be accepted by Thomas as they're likely also to be by any moderately knowledgeable and thoughtful reader.

Making the distinction makes possible the reconstrual of these objections so that they apply not to fear *simpliciter*, but only to a particular kind of it. What the distinction permits Thomas to do is accept both sides of a first-blush contradiction: that there is fear in heaven, and that it is not the case that there is fear in heaven. He needs to find a way to do that because affirmations of both sides are deeply rooted in the archive. The first two objections are grounded directly in scripture (Prv 1:33 and 1 Jn 3:2, respectively), as is the opposing view (Ps 19:9). The work the distinction does—nowhere described in these terms by Thomas—is that of permitting an internally-complex archive containing many first-blush contradictions to be read as internally consistent. That work is done: it's what this article does to and for the reader, how it appears to the reader. But the means of doing it—the conceptual distinction aimed at the reconciliation of difference—are, though explicitly present in the text (at the beginning of the *responsio*), not there explicitly flagged or identified in this way as having this function and purpose. The working of the distinction—how it works, and for what—remain among the features of the text invisible to the amateur reader. But they do become visible to readers who adopt the phenomenological attitude, and in becoming visible permit such readers to imitate and learn. Once this aspect of the article's working is manifest, it's easy enough to perform it—easy enough in principle, anyway, even if in practice demanding a conceptual subtlety and precision not widely available.

A second feature of this article, evident to those who adopt the phenomenological attitude and largely hidden from those who do not, is the work done by abstraction. The article is prompted, as are almost all those of the *ST*, by a brief and precise question: *utrum [timor] maneat in patria* (whether fear remains in heaven), which is responded to with the opening thesis: *videtur quod timor non remaneat in patria* (it seems that it doesn't). With question and (provisional) answer in hand, the article is off to the races. Both question and answer are laconic and highly abstract. There's a one-word subject, *timor*, left unglossed and uncommented upon; and there's a predicate clause (*[re]maneat in patria*) of like kind. Literary and conceptual exuberance are kept to a dry minimum in the article's setup, and this is entirely typical of Thomas in the *ST*, and mostly elsewhere. This abstraction is a surface and explicit feature of the text: the amateur reader will be at least inchoately aware of it. But the nature of the work done by this setup eludes such readers while it is evident and interesting to those who adopt the phenomenological attitude. That work is exactly to make possible the construction and deployment of the distinction at work in the *responsio*. Only if the question of the article is formulated in this fashion, without gloss or elaboration, can the reconciling work of the *responsio*'s *distinctiones* be performed. The setup's question-and-answer must be naked in order that the robing work of the distinction can be done. Seeing how this works permits imitation and replication in a way that staying with the article's explicit features does not.

A third aspect of the article's work evident to those who adopt the phenomenological attitude has to do with appeals to authority. (Almost) any reader of the article notices that Thomas quotes four pieces of scripture and identifies the scriptural books to which they belong (Psalms, Proverbs, 1 John), and three non-scriptural authorities, also with identification of the work from which the quotation comes (Gregory, *Moralia on Job*; Augustine, *City of God*; Pseudo-Dionysius, *Divine Names*). But readers who note these facts and are interested, if at all, principally in the substantive points Thomas uses the quotations to make, don't see what work the appeal to authority does, and thus aren't easily able to do that work in their own theological writing. What is the work done by appeal to—supportive and illustrative quotation of—authoritative sources? First, it displays (without explicitly noting) a feature of fundamental importance to Catholic intellectual work in general, and to theological work in particular: that is, its location in an archive of authorities. Catholic theological work cannot proceed without engaging itself with the archive as if it were authoritative. That is as true for the faithful, who believe that the archive indeed is authoritative, as for the pagan or the academic who do not take the archive to be authoritative, but nevertheless, if they are to do Catholic theology, must appeal to it as if it were and articulate their conclusions and speculations with it. The archive need not be present with the same degree of explicitness in the work of all Catholic theologians; but it is always there implicitly, and what it contains serves as a complex control on how theological work is done and what its conclusions are. Thomas's use of the archive in the article shows this clearly to those who've adopted the phenomenological attitude. It's very much less evident, if evident at all, to those with an eye principally to the particulars of the authorities he uses, and of the views attributed to them.

The presence of authorities in this article shows, however, much more than the mere fact of the archive-articulated nature of Catholic theological work. It shows also that the archive does not interpret itself—that what it says is sufficiently opaque or multivalent that it calls for interpretive resources which it does not itself provide. This is obvious enough as an *a priori*: no text—not scripture, not the canons of the ecumenical councils, not the most carefully framed and tightly defined encyclical or apostolic letter—provides all the resources needed for its own interpretation. But the bare *a priori* provides little formation for aspirant theologians who want and need to see how the archive may be used in theological work—who want, that is, fluency in that aspect of the theologian's work. The instance in this article of the *Summa* provides more. It shows to those who want to see what kind of work the archive may do that the archive's first-blush contradictions (for example, between Ps 19's affirmation that *timor dei* endures forever, and Prv 1's that in heaven there'll be abundance without fear) can be generative of thought, and perhaps that they should be sought out and thought about for exactly that reason. The interpretive assumption that Thomas deploys is (it seems; he doesn't display it here; its postulation serves to explain what he does, what the work of his quotations from scripture in the article is) that because the archive does not in fact contradict itself, its first-blush contradictions provide theologians with an opportunity for thought about what must, or might, be the case if what seems to be a contradiction actually isn't. Thomas's preferred device for such thinking is the distinction; it's not the only one, but it's a powerful one. Seeing it with clarity permits neophyte theologians to see how to deploy it themselves.

Lastly, for theologians seeking clarity about what work appeals to authority do in Thomas (or at least in this article), adopting the phenomenological attitude shows part of that work to be the provision of grammatical resources. The vocabulary (*timor, manere, patria*) of the authorities provides the lexicon Thomas uses, and their syntax—their proposals for combining those lexical items— gives him the materials for thought. Again, for readers seeking simply to know what Thomas thinks about whether there is fear in heaven, this work of the archive's authorities' presence in the *ST* remains invisible; but for those who adopt the phenomenological attitude because they aspire to theological fluency, it becomes evident. Differently put: this article's work is not only to recommend a pattern of thinking about fear in heaven, but also to show to its attuned and attentive readers an instance of theology as grammatical performance. In his response to the second objection (which is that because the LORD is fearless and we are conformed to the LORD when we are in heaven, we are therefore also fearless in heaven), Thomas writes that affirming the LORD's fearlessness doesn't require those who do it also to affirm the fearlessness of the blessed, intimate with and conformed to the LORD though they are, and that this is because the blessed remain subject to the LORD even in their blessedness, while the LORD is subject to no one. In writing that, Thomas makes a principally grammatical rather than a principally logical point. It is that fear of a certain sort and subjection go inseparably together: when one is mentioned the other must also be. That's a reminder of and an appeal to the fundamental and essential grammar of creatureliness, a grammar that marks the distinction between the LORD and everything that is not the LORD.

---

§30 PASTICHE AND (UN)ORIGINALITY

Those who make a practice of adopting the phenomenological attitude as they read theology—of looking closely at what's ordinarily looked through—find themselves increasingly able to compose theology, to confect theological texts themselves, because they see how it's done, how the texts they read do their work. That is the principal contribution of the phenomenological attitude to fluency: it yields, over time, increasing fluency in confection, which is among the things theologians need. Compositional fluency ought ideally be attained in more than one theological genre: the treatise, the polemic, the commentary, the *quaestio*, even the florilegium; and because this is so, attentive reading of a variety of genres, both within and without the phenomenological attitude, ought be practiced. It's not likely, however, that any theologian will find himself equally compositionally at home in all genres. Augustinians are likely to find themselves drawn to polemical theological writing, responsive as that typically is to particular opponents and particular challenges—their models might be the anti-Donatist or anti-Pelagian works of Augustine. Thomists will find their models, perhaps, in the *quaestio*-plus-*articulus* form of the *ST*, as also might Franciscan Scotists. Thomists are also likely to find the commentary genre attractive: it's remarkable how much of the broadly Thomist school has done its theology by way of commentary on Thomas's works (as he did some of his theology— Thomists will probably prefer to call it philosophy—by way of commentary on Aristotle's corpus), and how little of the Augustinian tradition's theological work has involved commentary on Augustine's corpus. Balthasar's lyrically dense essays and books—not exactly systematic, but more than occasional—provide another model, as do Lonergan's austere essays and treatises.

Fluency in theological composition has wide reading and the kind of attentiveness made possible by the phenomenological attitude among its necessary conditions. But such reading doesn't suffice. Aspiring theologians must also repeatedly practice composition, and the best way to do this, to begin with, is by pastiche. In this, as in so much else, theology is like any other practice: musical composition is learned in part by pastiche, as is composition in prose or poetry, and as is cookery. In the theological case, aspirants might begin by taking a model—Augustine's *De mendacio* (Lying), say; or Bonaventure's *Itinerarium mentis in deum* (The Mind's Journey into God); or a chapter of Thomas's *Summa contra Gentiles* (Summa Against the Gentiles); or one of Pascal's *Lettres provinciales* (Provincial Letters); or Mechthild of Magdeburg's *Das fließende Licht der Gottheit* (The Flowing Light of the Godhead); or Newman's "Tamworth Reading Room"; or ... the possibilities are almost endless. Whatever is chosen should be relatively brief. There's only futility in attempting a pastiche of the entire *De civitate dei* (City of God), or the entire *ST*. With a model in hand, the neophyte should read it several times, at first, intentionally, as an amateur reader would, with attention to the work's surface features, and then within the phenomenological attitude, letting the work's means of doing its work gradually show themselves. Gradually, the work's particularities will show themselves to the reader.

First, there are gross particularities, such as topic, diction, mood, voice, rhetorical tone, imagined or ideal reader, frame of reference, authorities and opponents mentioned, cited and quoted, and how this is done. Then there are implicit features of the text, such as the kind and degree of confidence the writer has in argument; what part the making of distinctions plays in the work's form; how incompleteness or puzzlement shape the work; how open or closed the fabric of the work's ratiocination is—and so on. Neophytes take note of all these things (it won't be easy: these are matters to which the mind has to force itself to attend, not matters that become smoothly evident); then, with the model clearly before them, they choose a topic or question different from, but like in kind and scope to, the one treated in their model; and they try to write a pastiche. If, for example, the model is Augustine's *De mendacio*, which treats what lying is and whether it is ever acceptable, aspiring theologians might pastiche it on the topic of insult or gossip understood as particular speech acts. If the model is the sixth of Pascal's *Lettres provinciales*, which treats, satirically, what he takes to be lax Jesuit casuistry on moral questions, such as whether a monk is permitted to go to a brothel for sex (answer: yes, so long as he's not wearing his habit); the neophyte might pastiche by writing a letter on the conditions under which a someone married might nonetheless be permitted—or even required—to commit adultery. These exercises are difficult, as difficult in their own way as imitating a Shakespearean sonnet or a Bach organ fugue. To do them well—to produce a work whose tone and form aren't easily distinguishable from those of the work being imitated, requires deep fluency. Repeated practice in such exercises, even if they're not done well at first, can produce just such fluency.

But don't pastiche-exercises like these make theology a derivative and imitative exercise? Aren't theologians who learn to do this like rock bands whose party pieces are note-for-note covers of numbers by the Beatles or the Rolling Stones? Doesn't this approach to learning how to be a theologian call originality and creativity into question? Yes and no. Originality and creativity are overrated virtues in every sphere of the intellectual life. Most intellectual work is and ought be deeply traditional in form and substance. This is especially true of Catholic theological work, whose resonance with and conformity to its archive is an essential characteristic. But it is true that if pastiche were the only thing theologians were called upon to do, these criticisms would to some degree be justified. Those pastiche-exercises, however, are high-level preparations, not the thing itself. Theologians, now no longer exactly neophytes but something closer to adepts, who can, at call, write substantively interesting theological work in the style of and according to the norms of work done by any half-dozen of the *doctores ecclesiae*, have effectively completed their training. They've a high degree of fluency and are ready to develop a style—if they feel its need—distinctively different from any previously used. Some few of them may be ready to write preludes and fugues as original as Chopin's were for his time, even though they've learned to do that, as Chopin did, by close study of and pastiche upon, those of Bach. Not many theologians will achieve that; few living theologians (certainly not this one) would be able to perform even the pastiche exercises mentioned, much less compose as a virtuoso.

The value of such exercises shouldn't be underestimated, even though they are essentially imitative.

---

§31 HABIT, TECHNIQUE, GRACE

Doesn't all this emphasis on the development of theological fluency make being a theologian just like being an orchestral composer, a gardener, an automechanic, or a stock trader? That is, a matter of remorseless work to develop particular skills, and then of more work to deploy those skills in the composition of texts? And doesn't this in turn demean theology, making it into a worldly work and removing any need for the grace to which in fact theologians ought always be responding? Yes on all counts, except that to understand the accrual of fluency in this way is not at all to demean theology or remove it from grace and grace from it. Fluency in theology is just like fluency in anything else. It requires work and the establishment of habits. This doesn't at all mean that it's not responsive to grace, or properly to be categorized as an idolatrous activity because it involves grace's refusal. Rather—and again this doesn't differentiate theology from anything else—when theology is done well, the agency of those who do it is fully articulated with and non-competitively responsive to the LORD's agency. When badly done, its errors and lacks and incompletenesses are exactly the places where the agency of the theologian has full and autonomous control of what's produced. Sin is the only thing we do autonomously, as laws to ourselves; sin's analogue in the intellectual life is self-directed error, and of that we're all abundantly capable, more than we can know or easily say.

Even unbelieving extra-ecclesial theologians are responsive to and cooperative with grace when they do good theology—when, that is, what they say and write about the LORD is true, corrective of error, provocative of further and better theological talk and writing, and the like. Such theologians are unlikely to consider that what they do is responsive, and so forth, to grace, while at the same time knowing, if Catholic theology is what they're doing, that it belongs to those fluent in that discourse to say things of that kind. But this is irrelevant to the question of whether in fact the theological work they do is responsive to grace. Performance and providing an account of performance are distinct skills with few and distant causal connections.

---

§32 QUESTION, DISTINCTION, JUXTAPOSITION, ELUCIDATION

Reading in the archive (deep, broad, repeated, within and without the phenomenological attitude, under explicit guidance and not), and pastiche exercises on representative works from the archive: these are the generic practices that produce theological fluency. There are also more particular skills, needed to some degree by all theologians but not to an identical degree by all. These include: making and deploying conceptual distinctions; identifying and using questions; and imagining and responding to objections to a position speculatively taken or entertained. The thought experiment is a device of importance to all these. By means of it, a performance of the conceptual imagination, distinctions hitherto not in play can be identified, questions to order and drive speculation on a theological topic can be defined and polished, and arguments honed, ramified, and brought into hand-to-hand combat with another. The intellectual life in a devastated world is necessarily agonistic, even if not necessarily antagonistic. Theological work is no exception. How are these more particular skills to be developed?

Theological work, like most intellectual work, is question-driven. That is, formulating a good question is requisite to theological speculation. In knowing what to ask lies the capacity to develop the church's understanding of its doctrine. Skill at formulating questions is, therefore, among the habits speculative theologians need to work at developing. It's a skill intimate with that of making conceptual distinctions: faced with a lexical item of central importance to the grammar of the faith, distinction-makers look for ways to fine-tune it; suggesting such ways almost inevitably yields questions. Consider, for example, "grace" (*charis*, *gratia*, and so on). The distinction-maker divides it into kinds (universal, actual, sufficient, operative, superadded, and so on), and is thereby led to questions, such as: are there kinds of grace available only to the baptized? Is there anything exempt from grace? How is grace related to nature? How ought prevenient grace (the grace that comes before, comes first), be related to the (putative) freedom of the (putatively) natural human being? And so on. Each of these questions has been generative in the history of Christian theology, which is not to say that each of them has been decisively—doctrinally—answered, or that all of them are always generative. Some questions are, after a time, exhausted, having yielded all they can by way of provocation to the work of theology. Theologians' distinction-making skills are likely to develop in symbiosis with their question-formulating skills. Both ought be attended to and cultivated.

Distinctions aren't the only devices that yield good—fecund—theological questions. Another device, equally productive, is the juxtaposition of claims from one sphere of Christian discourse with claims from another that seem at first blush distant from one another. Consider, for instance, the dogmatic claim that Mary is immaculate, meaning without sin, whether inherited or committed. Consider, also, the (almost) doctrinal claim that death has sin among its necessary conditions. The first claim belongs to mariology; the second to Christian theological anthropology and cosmology. Juxtaposing them at once yields the question: did Mary die? If she is truly exempt from sin, and if sin really is a necessary condition for death, then perhaps she didn't. But if sin has meanings that permit those not individually subject to it nonetheless to be subject to death, then perhaps she did. And (or) if "death" isn't a univocal term as it applies to human creatures (to which category Mary indisputably belongs), then perhaps she did. Perhaps, too, there are reasons for (and a causal nexus that explains) Mary's death that are in her case quite independent of sin. The church has no doctrine on this matter, and speculative theologians differ about it; the question is, though, generative, and it is produced by juxtaposition.

There's a third way, too, in which good theological questions can be generated. Take one or another settled doctrinal claim from the archive; or, take a claim broadly agreed by Catholic speculative theologians. Then apply to it a device of thought not itself derived from the archive but rather part of the general inheritance of pagan thought in which Christians also share, with an eye to the engendering of theological questions (or distinctions) not previously considered. One such device, an ordinary part of modal logic with nothing especially Christian about it, is the distinction between necessity and possibility. If a claim is necessarily true, then it could not fail to be true in any possible world; its denial is a contradiction. For example: *everything other than the LORD is a creature*. If a claim is true, but contingently so, then the state of affairs it indicates could have been otherwise: for example, *Augustine died in 430 A.D.* That means its mode is possibility: it's actually true, but might not have been; it's not incoherent to deny it, even though its denial is false.

Suppose this device is applied to a theological claim that approaches doctrinal status, such as, *it is not the case that everyone is saved*. Such application yields two possibilities: *necessarily it is not the case that everyone is saved*; and, *possibly it is not the case that everyone is saved*. The realization that there are these two possibilities at once yields questions. The most obvious among these is: which of these derived claims is, first, coherent with the initial claim (*it is not the case that everyone is saved*), and, second, true? It's reasonable to say that each of the derived claims is compatible with the initial claim. The first, the one produced by application of the necessity-operator, says something considerably stronger than the initial claim; and the second is compatible with both the initial claim and its denial. Further consideration yields all sorts of interesting possibilities; my own opinion, speculative of course (it can be nothing else; there's no doctrine on the question), is that *possibly it is not the case that everyone is saved* is the correct specification of the initial *it is not the case that everyone is saved*, and that it's important to see that it entails (is exchangeable with) the claim that *possibly it is the case that everyone is saved*. If correct, this means that the proper speculative position to take on the question of universalism—the question of whether everyone is saved—is to say that it's possibly true, and, therefore, possibly false. This judgment is found as a minority position within the tradition. The majority positions are, first, that the initial claim should be left in the indicative mood, which means that universalism's denial is contingently false; and, second, that universalism's denial is necessarily true. The application of a simple logical device to a theological claim generates questions about it which would otherwise be difficult to see.

These methods of generating questions—the making of conceptual distinctions; juxtaposition of claims from one sphere of theological discourse with claims from another; application to theological positions of conceptual devices drawn from without the tradition—ought each be attended to and practiced by theologians-in-training. Exercises in their deployment ought form part of theological training, as complements to those in reading and pastiche. Fecundity in question development is a mark of theological virtuosity; like anything else, it can be practiced and developed.

§33 AGONISM, ANTAGONISM, ARGUMENT

Agon is Greek for struggle; agonism is engagement in struggle. All intellectual life has the *agon* at its core because all of it involves the making and defense of distinctions, which is necessarily agonistic. Without the *agon* in that sense, there is no intellectual life, and indeed no thought. Language itself classifies and orders the world, and its users—all of us—have constantly to struggle to align the world with linguistic distinctions and to adapt such distinctions to the world. Thought about a particular topic—the LORD, say—intensifies and elaborates that kind of agonism. Theology has been practiced largely by the offering, defense, elaboration, and retractation of conceptual distinctions. It could not have been otherwise; it cannot be otherwise.

Agonism, however, is not antagonism. An antagonist is an opponent, a particular other whose conclusions and distinctions and arguments stand opposed to yours, or seem to do so. The (perceived or real) presence of antagonists requires argument under the sign of polemic; what antagonists hope for when they engage one another is victory, as much as clarification and learning. Much theology, like much intellectual life, is antagonistic as well as agonistic, but not all of it is. Agonism is an inward pressure, a characteristic feature of thought; antagonism is an occasional external need, common but not essential. For some theologians (certainly for this one) antagonism is something like a need: for them, the presence of an opponent and a challenge is a necessary occasion for thought. But this is in large part a matter of temperament. Not all theologians need antagonists, and for those who don't, theological thought can proceed agonistically without being antagonistic.

Nonetheless, argument, understood as the performance of polemic, is something that theologians need to know how to do. The Christian-theological archive shows, abundantly, the importance of explicitly antagonistic argument to the development of theological thinking: Athanasius against the Arians, Augustine against the Pelagians, Thomas against the Averroists, Pascal against the Jesuits, Newman against the liberals ... the list of theological polemicists is long and distinguished. Theological polemic has in some respects become less attractive to Catholic theologians, ecclesial and otherwise, in our time, but there is no good, principled reason to downplay its significance. Rather, it's exactly because of its reduced prominence that neophyte theologians now need to have their attention directed toward it more explicitly and directly than toward some of the other skills they need.

Argument may be against an imaginary opponent. In such a case, theologians consider the thesis they're entertaining or speculating about, and construct the strongest objections to it they can come up with. They shouldn't do this insouciantly, confident that their initial position is right and that all objections to it can be met; rather, they ought to do it, as best they can, in an attempt to inhabit the thought of someone who might find their position unacceptable, and in that way to see what arguments might be put forward for its unacceptability. For example: suppose you're inclined to think that it properly belongs to Catholic theology to say that the nonhuman created order—all animate and inanimate creatures other than humans (and angels; but they can be left aside for the purposes of this example), that is—exists solely for the benefit of human creatures, that it is ordered to and for them in something analogically like the way that human creatures are ordered to and for the LORD. That is certainly a possible and rather widely held Catholic position. If you are inclined to hold it, speculatively (I'm not), then, as someone concerned to develop argumentative skill, you should, at various points in your thought and writing about the matter, pause, exit, to the extent that you can, your train of thought together with its assumptions and entailments, and enter that of someone for whom the conclusion you're entertaining is speculatively improper.

Inhabiting that mode of thought, you'd work to see what the assumptions are that make it seem improper, what opposed positions those assumptions suggest—perhaps they'd include the claim that *the nonhuman order glorifies the LORD independently of relations it bears to the human order*—and what the arguments are that might be brought to bear *pro* and *contra*. You'd do this disinterestedly, engaging in a genuine attempt to see where the argument goes and how deep the disagreement is. You'd likely find that differences on a variety of topics in theological anthropology, theological cosmology, and (probably) trinitarian theology would surface, and that the arguments *pro* and *contra* would rapidly ramify. At some point you'd leave this thought experiment behind, perhaps by now half convinced that the position you've been exploring is preferable to the one you began with, and return to the first position. You'll now have a much clearer sense of what's at stake, and the depth of what's at stake, than you had before; and you'll be equipped to pursue the argument with zest. Old-fashioned English Marxists used to advocate exercises of this sort in order to clarify differences; there are analogous practices encouraged in the debate-centered curricula of some Tibetan Buddhist monastic schools; and formal high-school debates, at a rather less elevated level, recommend something similar. The upshot is, or can be, a clarity of thought produced by argument-inflected accentuation of difference. This is something that every theologian should want; developing skill in it is something that should be part of every theological curriculum.

But imaginary opponents aren't the best kind. Vastly preferable in most cases are real ones. They're much more likely to come up with arguments against your position which you haven't the energy or the imagination to construct for yourself; and their thought will have a style-signature in principle unavailable to you because of the difference between their formation and yours. This is the truly productive argumentative situation, and it should be sought out: it can produce a clarification of differences much broader and deeper than that given by imagining opponents. It's one of the significant failings of most Catholic theological training, whether seminary-centered, university-based, or occurring in a house of religious formation, that it rarely provides engagement with representatives of positions foreign or opposed to the lineage being transmitted in a particular place, and even more rarely endorses the importance of these as part of theological formation. This should change. Theologians, ecclesial or otherwise, think and write better about the LORD when they have to engage, argumentatively, the particulars of their thought with those of other schools of theology or other theologians.

Skill in argument and skill in the development of questions are intimate one with another. Good theological questions lead to good theological arguments, and good arguments typically generate good questions. Each is nurtured by opposition as much as—usually more than—by agreement or the softhanded leading of the nurturer. This is another reason why theology ought to be construed broadly, as in this book. Extra-ecclesial theologians, whether pagans or academics, are much more likely to offer ecclesial theologians arguments and questions they'd not have thought of by themselves than are other ecclesial theologians; and it's among the advantages of the understanding of theology offered in this book that it makes it easier for ecclesial theologians to recognize that their non-ecclesial counterparts are engaged in a variant of their own enterprise, and therefore to engage them and learn from them. It's a mark of a degenerating intellectual enterprise that it lacks the conceptual resources and energy to make possible serious engagement with those who don't belong to it. The more narrowly theology is understood, and the more qualifications— virtue, sanctity, baptismal status, faith, and so on—added to who may count as a theologian, the less likely it is that sharp distinctions, good questions, and difference-clarifying arguments will be offered.

§34 DISCOVERY, INTERPRETATION, SPECULATION

The theologian's skills are those proper to any intellectual enterprise: appropriate depth and range of relevant knowledge, obtained in the case of Catholic theology by knowledge of the archive, and appropriate levels of skill in deploying knowledge in the service of theological speculation. Particular to the case of Catholic theology is the use of this knowledge and these skills in accordance with a threefold schema: discovery, interpretation, and speculation.

First among these, in the order of analysis and usually in the order of practice as well, is discovery. The first thing Catholic theologians need to do in considering a particular theological question or topic is discovery of what counts as doctrine with respect to it—what, that is, constitutes the church's lexicon and substantive teaching with respect to it. That lexicon and that teaching bind them: they are the material upon which their thought works. To be a theologian is to be under authority: the authority, most fundamentally, of the LORD's self-revelation, which means, textually speaking, the authority of scripture and of magisterially given teaching, which is itself formulated under the direct guidance of the Spirit.

This task of discovery is often no easy one. The tradition is long, its archive large and in many languages, and the relative authoritative weight of its various elements itself a matter of doctrine, and, therefore, of interpretive dispute. Once discovered, the content of what has been discovered needs to be ordered and systematized to the extent possible and appropriate to whatever question is under consideration. Then, theologians know, always imperfectly and often erroneously, what they have to deal with. They know the liberating constraints under which their thought may now work—rather as trial lawyers, once the process of legal discovery is complete, know what they have to work with, what is possible in the way of argument and what is not, and how the case may now be constructed. Discovery is followed by interpretation. No doctrine, whether scriptural, conciliar, or more broadly magisterial, interprets itself; there are always many suggestions that can be made about how a doctrine may be read; and it is a proper part of the theologian's task to make just such suggestions.

Very often, a particular theologian's suggestions as to how this or that doctrine ought be interpreted will be pursued by juxtaposition: that is, deciding which doctrines to juxtapose to which influences how they are read—it pushes interpretive thought about them in a certain direction. But this is not the only way to perform the task of interpretation. Theologians may also look for points of doctrinal tension within the broadly magisterial tradition and suggest speculative resolutions of them: about, for example, the weight and significance of the thought of Thomas Aquinas for determining the theological import of particular philosophical positions, or about whether there is any need for a theologian to think that there is a meaningful distinction between theology and philosophy, or about whether the fairly consistent magisterial denial of bodies to the angels entails that they have no spacetime location.

It's also possible, and perhaps this is the most common case, to look at some widely distributed element of the magisterial lexicon whose semantic content and syntax are underinterpreted, or whose interpretation is controversial, such as "own body" (*corpus proprium*) being said of both the flesh of a particular person before death and after the general resurrection; or *subsistit in*, said of the relation between the church of Jesus Christ and the visible Catholic church; or *persona* used as a term of art for Father, Son, and Spirit; and then to suggest some ways of thinking about what these terms or phrases mean, and how they might be combined with others.

This is by no means an exhaustive list of the ways in which theologians' interpretive task may be undertaken. It is an essential and many-faceted aspect of what the theologian is called upon to do, and it is ingenuity and energy in performing the interpretive task that largely distinguishes great theologians from merely good ones.

Discovery and interpretation are followed by speculation. For me, and I suspect for many theologians, theology's speculative aspect is its most interesting and intellectually exciting. That's not because I expect to arrive at the truth by theological speculation, though of course I hope for that; neither is it because I think that the understandings of particular topics I entertain when I speculate theologically have any authority, or indeed any weight at all other than that to be found in the responses they might prompt in others who read them, and the effect they might have, utterly imponderable, on the deliberations of the teaching church over time. Speculation is, rather, a delight because it is something close to a pure activity of the intellect, an unadulterated thought-performance about matters of great importance—matters of greater importance than all others. When theologians speculate, they begin to move beyond doctrine. That is because, if the tasks of discovery and interpretation have been done well, the theologian knows what doctrine requires on this matter, and has at least begun the task of interpreting and ordering the *depositum fidei*.

§35 THEOLOGICAL WORK AND CHURCH DOCTRINE

Discovery, interpretation, and speculation are the theologian's central tasks; the establishment of church doctrine does not belong to the list. It is not what theologians do. It is, instead, essentially an episcopal function. Theologians may and should teach church doctrine by ordering it, systematizing it, writing books and essays in which it is set forth, giving lectures on it, speculating about it, and so on. But that is not the same as establishing what the church's doctrine is. Doing that requires an authority theologians lack: the authority to pronounce, performatively, on the question of what it is that the church teaches about this or that, and in the act of pronouncing to make it so. Historians and analysts of the baseball book of rules may certainly depict, analyze, and offer speculative suggestions about the definitions of "ball" and "strike"; but they have no power to rule on the field of play that some pitch is one or the other. That power is reserved to umpires, and it is a performative power: when the umpire calls a strike, that act suffices to make it one; when the church's bishops assembled define doctrine, that act suffices to make it such, and it does so because of the guidance and inspiration of the Holy Spirit. There are, of course, complications here on questions of detail: it is not always clear just when the church's bishops have defined doctrine; and the category "doctrine" itself is internally complex—there are kinds and degrees. But the schema given remains valid and important even if it is not always easy to see just how to apply it. Clarifying its application is among the tasks of theologians.

Clarity about the nondoctrinal nature of theological work is, or ought to be, productive of speculative work of a daring and radical kind. If it is incumbent upon theologians to get as clear as they can about the difference between church doctrine, on the one hand, and speculative proposals about and elaborations of doctrine, on the other, then theologians are freed from anxiety about whether their speculative proposals are right. It is not up to them—to us—to decide this; whether any element of a particular theologian's speculative proposal is incorporated into church doctrine is a decision made by the teaching church over time, with the college of bishops playing an essential role in arriving at that decision. And usually the time taken is so much that the theologian is safely dead and (perhaps) enjoying a preliminary version of the beatific vision before it is clear how his work has been appropriated and used by the church. In this way, theologians are relieved of anxiety about their own rightness and their own influence, at least if they are Catholic; the picture is very different for Protestant theologians, on whose shoulders a heavy weight is placed, one that cannot be borne and that hampers and constrains the properly speculative aspect of theological work. The same weight bears down upon Catholic theologians when they forget, or avert their gaze from, the nature of their task. What we have as Catholic theologians is the deep freedom that comes from the recognition of the authority under which we work.

---

§36 THEOLOGY DEFINED: CODA

Theology is reasoned discourse about god (or the gods) aimed at cognitive intimacy with what it's about. Theology's Christian instance is reasoned discourse about the god who is the triune LORD, the god of Israel who become incarnate as Jesus the Christ. Its goal is the same: cognitive intimacy, to the extent possible, with the LORD it's about. On this understanding of theology, the Christian instance of it is a doubly open field: it's open in one direction to anyone who wishes to perform it by gaining the necessary knowledge and skill; and it's open in the other direction to learning whatever can be learned from those who perform theology extra-ecclesially. The church, the sacrament of the world, opens itself to any who wish to work at its theology, whether or not they are members of Christ's body; and it receives instruction and inspiration from those who perform as theologians in communities and traditions external to itself. In those ways, the LORD is glorified, and the endless enterprise, delightful in itself and beautiful in its offerings, of increasing cognitive intimacy with the LORD, is fructified.

§37 WHAT TO DO NEXT

This is a how-to book for aspiring Catholic theologians. What such theologians need is, the book has suggested, a body of knowledge and a set of skills. Both the knowledge and the skills are, in considerable part, acquired and sharpened by reading. Aspiring theologians, therefore, need some guidance about what to read. What follows is exactly such guidance, divided into three parts. First, a list of the thirty-six *doctores ecclesiae*, together with a brief note on each intended to help the aspiring theologian identify which among them might be most useful as an interlocutor, and which among each *doctor*'s works might be good to begin with. Second, a list of the works that should belong to every theologian's reference library; they should be easily available, preferably within arm's reach, and often consulted. Third, a highly selective list of works that treat topics also treated in this book, mostly, though by no means exclusively, from a perspective at odds with the one adopted here. Editions and translations mentioned in each of these three lists have primary reference to the United States; theologians working in other countries, whether English-using or not, should modify the list accordingly. Many of the printed editions mentioned are also available in electronic formats and in online versions, and while the usual care should be exercised in using such versions, they are, increasingly, the point of first reference, and they have the enormous advantage of making the practice of Catholic theology possible for those without access to research libraries.

§38 *DOCTORES ECCLESIAE*

There are, at the time of this writing (2015), thirty-six doctors of the church. The following list is arranged chronologically by birth date. Each entry contains the doctor's name, years of birth and death (many of which, especially for the early doctors, are approximate, and some of which are disputed) followed by the year in which the person was declared a *doctor ecclesiae*, and then a sentence or two about the person and his or her work.

1. Athanasius [of Alexandria] (296–373, 1568). Bishop of Alexandria and defender of orthodoxy against Arianism. Principal works: *On the Incarnation*; *Defense Against the Arians*; *Life of Anthony*.

2. Ephrem [the Syrian] (306–73, 1920). Deacon, catechist, hymnographer, poet, biblical commentator, apologist. Principal works: *Commentary on the Diatesseron*; *On Virginity*; *The Homily on Our Lord*; *Letter to Publius*.

3. Hilary [of Poitiers] (312–67, 1851). Bishop of Poitiers and defender of orthodoxy against Arianism. Principal works: *Commentary on the Gospel of Matthew*; *The Trinity*; *The Synods*.

4. Cyril [of Jerusalem] (313–86, 1883). Bishop of Jerusalem, catechist. Principal work: *Catechetical Lectures*.

5. Basil [of Caesarea] (330–79, 1568). Bishop of Caesarea, biblical exegete, trinitarian theologian. Principal works: *Treatise on the Holy Spirit*; *The Six Days of Creation*; *Against Eunomius*.

6. Gregory [of Nazianzus] (330–89, 1568). Archbishop of Constantinople, also known as Gregory the Theologian; preacher, poet, orator, theologian. Principal works: *Theological Orations*; *Festal Orations*; *Poemata arcana*.

7. Ambrose [of Milan] (339–97, 1298). Bishop of Milan, baptizer of Augustine, biblical exegete, hymnographer, theologian. Principal works: *On Duties*; *On the Birth of the Virgin and the Perpetual Virginity of Mary*; *Explanation of the Psalms*.

8. John Chrysostom (345–407, 1568). Archbishop of Constantinople, reformer, liturgist, biblical exegete, preacher. Principal works: *On the Priesthood*; *On the Incomprehensibility of God*; *On the Baptism of Christ*.

9. Jerome (347–420, 1298). Priest, monk, papal secretary, biblical exegete and commentator, polemicist, linguist, translator. Principal works: *Against the Pelagians*; *Against Jovinian; Book of Illustrious Men*.

10. Augustine [of Hippo] (354–430, 1298). Bishop of Hippo, philosopher, theologian, apologist, preacher. Principal works: *Confessions*; *The Trinity*; *City of God*.

11. Cyril [of Alexandria] (378–444, 1883). Patriarch of Alexandria, theologian. Principal works: *That Christ is One*; *Five Books Against Nestorius*.

12. Leo [the Great] (390–461, 1754). Pope, theologian. Principal work: *Tome*.

13. Peter Chrysologus (406–50, 1729). Bishop of Ravenna, preacher. His principal works are his surviving sermons.

14. Gregory [the Great] (540–604, 1298). Pope, liturgist, theologian, exegete. Principal works: *Book of Pastoral Rule*; *Dialogues*; *Morals on Job*.

15. Isidore [of Seville] (560–636, 1722). Archbishop of Seville, encyclopedist, theologian. Principal works: *Etymologies*; *The Nature of Things*.

16. Bede [the Venerable] (673–735, 1899). Monk, historian, linguist, exegete, theologian, reformer of the calendar. Principal works: *Ecclesiastical History of the English People*; *Martyrology*; *Time*; *The Reckoning of Time*.

17. John [of Damascus] (675–749, 1899). Monk, priest, theologian, hymnographer. Principal works: *On the Divine Image*; *Fountain of Wisdom*; *On Heresies*.

18. Gregory [of Narek] (951–1003, 2015). Monk, priest, biblical commentator, mystical philosopher, poet. Principal works: *Book of Prayer*; *Commentary on Song of Songs*.

19. Peter Damian (1007–72, 1828). Cardinal, bishop of Ostia, monk, ascetic, papal legate, reformer, theologian. Principal works: *Divine Omnipotence*; *Book of Gomorrah*.

20. Anselm [of Canterbury] (1033–1109, 1720). Archbishop, abbot, monk, philosopher. Principal works: *Monologion*; *Proslogion*; *Why God Became Man*; *Truth*.

21. Bernard [of Clairvaux] (1090–1153, 1830). Monk, abbot, mystic, biblical exegete. Principal works: *Sermons on the Song of Songs*; *On Grace and Free Will*; *The Love of God*.

22. Hildegard [of Bingen] (1098–1179, 2012). Nun, abbess, mystic, visionary, naturalist, botanist, composer, playwright. Principal works: *Scivias*; *Book of Life's Merits*; *Book of Divine Works*.

23. Anthony [of Padua] (1195–1231, 1946). Priest, monk, preacher, biblical exegete, teacher. Principal work: *Sermons for Feast Days*.

24. Albert [the Great] (1200–1280, 1931). Bishop, monk, scientist, biblical exegete, philosopher, theologian, teacher of Thomas Aquinas. Principal works: *Treatise on Man*; *Summa of Theology*.

25. Bonaventure (1221–74, 1588). Cardinal, bishop, monk, philosopher, biblical exegete, preacher, theologian. Principal works: *Commentary on the Sentences*; *The Mind's Road to God*.

26. Thomas Aquinas (1224–74, 1568). Priest, friar, philosopher, theologian. Principal works: *Summa of Theology*; *Summa against the Gentiles*; *Commentary on the Sentences*.

27. Catherine [of Siena] (1347–80, 1970). Nun, papal legate, teacher, mystic. Principal work: *The Dialogue of Divine Providence*.

28. John [of Avila] (1500–1569, 2012). Priest, missionary, preacher, biblical commentator, theologian, mystic, catechist. Principal works: *Listen, Daughter*; *Reform of the Ecclesiastical State*; *Treatise on the Love of God*.

29. Teresa [of Avila] (1515–82, 1970). Nun, reformer, mystic, theologian, poet, ascetic. Principal works: *The Interior Castle*; *Way of Perfection*; *Life*.

30. Peter Canisius (1521–97, 1925). Priest, religious, teacher, theologian, defender of Catholicism against Protestantism. Principal works: *A Summary of Christian Teaching*; *A Little Catechism for Catholics*.

31. John [of the Cross] (1542–91, 1926). Priest, friar, mystic, poet, theologian. Principal works: *Dark Night of the Soul*; *The Ascent of Mount Carmel*; *Living Flame of Love*.

32. Robert Bellarmine (1542–1621, 1931). Cardinal, priest, teacher, papal advisor. Principal works: *Disputations; The Seven Words of Christ; The Art of Dying Well.*

33. Laurence [of Brindisi] (1559–1619, 1959). Monk, papal nuncio, linguist, exegete, Counter-Reformation theologian. Principal works: *Image of Lutheranism; Commentary on Genesis; Sermons.*

34. Francis de Sales (1567–1622, 1877). Bishop of Geneva, spiritual director, Counter-Reformation theologian. Principal works: *Introduction to the Devout Life; The Love of God.*

35. Alphonsus Liguori (1696–1787, 1871). Bishop of Sant'Agata dei Goti, composer, philosopher, moral theologian, mariologist. Principal works: *Moral Theology; The Glories of Mary.*

36. Thérèse [of Lisieux] (1873–97, 1997). Nun, mystic, poet, theologian. Principal work: *Story of a Soul.*

---

§39 THE THEOLOGIAN'S WORKING LIBRARY

Beal, John P., et al., eds. *New Commentary on the Code of Canon Law.* Washington, D.C.: Canon Law Society of America, 2000.

Biblia Sacra Iuxta Vulgatam Versionem. Edited by Robert Weber et al. 5th ed. Stuttgart: Deutsche Bibelgesellschaft, 2007.

Catechism of the Catholic Church. 2nd rev. ed. Washington, D.C.: United States Catholic Conference, 1997.

Codex Iuris Canonici / Code of Canon Law. Latin/English edition. Washington, D.C.: Canon Law Society of America, 1983.

Congregation for the Doctrine of the Faith. "Donum Veritatis. An Instruction on the Ecclesial Vocation of the Theologian." Promulgated in 1990. Text available in several languages from www.vatican.va.

Denzinger, Heinrich, et al. *Enchiridion symbolorum definitionum et declarationum de rebus fidei et morum / Compendium of Creeds, Definitions, and Declarations on Matters of Faith and Morals.* 43rd ed. San Francisco, Calif.: Ignatius Press, 2012.

International Theological Commission. "Theology Today: Perspective, Principles and Criteria." A document issued in 2012. Text available in several languages from www.vatican.va.

Neuner, Josef, and Jacques Dupuis, eds. and trans. *The Christian Faith in the Doctrinal Documents of the Catholic Church*. 7th ed. New York: Alba House, 2001.

Nova Vulgata Bibliorum Sacrorum Editio. Rome: Libreria Editrice Vaticana, 1979.

Pelikan, Jaroslav. *Credo: Historical and Theological Guide to Creeds and Confessions of Faith in the Christian Tradition*. New Haven, Conn.: Yale University Press, 2003.

Pietersma, Albert, and Benjamin G. Wright, eds. *A New English Translation of the Septuagint and the Other Greek Translations Traditionally Included Under That Title*. Oxford: Oxford University Press, 2007.

Rites of the Catholic Church. 2 vols. Collegeville, Minn.: Pueblo, 1990–91.

Scripture—(1) For all: manual editions of the Hebrew text of the Old Testament, the Greek text of the Septuagint, the Greek text of the New Testament, the Vulgate (cf. *Biblia Sacra Iuxta Vulgatam*, in this list), the New Vulgate (cf. *Nova Vulgata*, in this list). (2) For English-using theologians: manual editions of the Revised Standard Version (Catholic edition), the New American Bible, the New Jerusalem Bible, and the New International Version. See also: Swift, *Vulgate*; Pietersma et al., *Septuagint* in this list.

Swift, Edgar, et al., eds. and trans. *The Vulgate Bible*. 6 vols. Dumbarton Oaks Medieval Library. Cambridge, Mass.: Harvard University Press, 2010–13.

Tanner, Norman P., ed. and trans. *Decrees of the Ecumenical Councils*. 2 vols. London / Washington, D.C.: Sheed and Ward / Georgetown University Press, 1990.

Ashley, Matthew J., et al. "Teaching Catholic Theology in the Coming Decade." *Horizons* 37, no. 2 (2010): 292–326.

Balthasar, Hans Urs von. "The Place of Theology." In his *Explorations in Theology 1: The Word Made Flesh*, translated by A. V. Littledale, 149–60. San Francisco, Calif.: Ignatius Press, 1989.

———. "Theology and Sanctity." In his *Explorations in Theology 1: The Word Made Flesh*, translated by A. V. Littledale, 181–209. San Francisco, Calif.: Ignatius Press, 1989.

Bonaventure. *De reductione artium ad theologiam* (Reduction of the Arts to Theology). Translated by Zacahary Hayes as *St. Bonaventure's On the Reduction of the Arts to Theology*. St. Bonaventure, New York: Franciscan institute, 1996.

Butler, Sara. "Theology Today: What Constitutes Catholic Theology?" *Chicago Studies* 52, no. 1 (2013): 66–79.

Cessario, Romanus. "Scholarship and Sanctity: A Lesson Aquinas Teaches the Priest and Seminarian." In his *Theology and Sanctity*, edited by Cajetan Cuddy, 151–79. Ave Maria, Fla.: Sapientia Press, 2014.

Doran, Robert M. *What Is Systematic Theology?* Toronto: University of Toronto Press, 2005.

Dulles, Avery, et al. "Catholicism 101: Challenges to a Theological Education." *Horizons* 33, no. 2 (2006): 303–29.

Griffiths, Paul J. *Intellectual Appetite: A Theological Grammar*. Washington, D.C.: The Catholic University of America Press, 2009.

Komonchak, Joseph A. "The Future of Theology in the Church." In *New Horizons in Theology*, edited by Terrence W. Tilley, 16–39. Maryknoll, N.Y.: Orbis, 2005.

Lacoste, Jean-Yves. *From Theology to Theological Thinking*. Translated by W. Chris Hackett. Charlottesville: University of Virginia Press, 2014.

Marshall, Bruce. "Quod Scit Una Uetula: Aquinas on the Nature of Theology." In *The Theology of Thomas Aquinas*, edited by Joseph

Wawrykow and Rik Van Nieuwenhove, 1–35. Notre Dame, Ind.: University of Notre Dame Press, 2005.

———. "The Ecclesial Vocation of the Theologian." In *A Man of the Church: Honoring the Theology, Life, and Witness of Ralph del Colle*, edited by Michael René Barnes, 23–39. Eugene, Ore.: Wipf & Stock, 2012.

McGinn, Bernard. *The Doctors of the Church: Thirty-Three Men and Women Who Shaped Christianity*. New York: Crossroad, 2009.

Murdoch, Jessica. "On the Relationship between Sanctity and Knowledge: Holiness as an Epistemological Criterion in St. Thomas." *Pro Ecclesia* 23, no. 4 (2014): 418–34.

Nichols, Aidan. *The Shape of Catholic Theology: An Introduction to Its Sources, Principles, and History*. Collegeville, Minn.: Liturgical Press, 1991.

O'Collins, Gerald. *Rethinking Fundamental Theology*. Oxford: Oxford University Press, 2013.

Piderit, John, and Melanie Morey, eds. *Teaching the Tradition: Catholic Themes in Academic Disciplines*. New York: Oxford University Press, 2012.

Ratzinger, Joseph. *Principles of Catholic Theology: Building Stones for a Fundamental Theology*. San Francisco, Calif.: Ignatius Press, 1987.

———. *The Nature and Mission of Theology: Approaches to Understanding Its Role in the Light of Present Controversy*. San Francisco, Calif.: Ignatius Press, 1995.

Rigali, Norbert. "The Ecclesial Responsibilities of Theologians, Forty Years after Vatican II." *Horizons* 33, no. 2 (2006): 298–302.

Sertillanges, A. G. *The Intellectual Life: Its Spirit, Conditions, Methods*. Translated by Mary Ryan. Washington, D.C.: The Catholic University of America Press, 1987.

Williams, A. N. *The Architecture of Theology: Structure, System, and Ratio*. Oxford: Oxford University Press, 2011.

The Practice of Catholic Theology: A Modest Proposal was designed in Scala Sans with Minion Pro display type and composed by Kachergis Book Design of Pittsboro, North Carolina. It was printed on 60-pound Natural Eggshell and bound by McNaughton & Gunn of Saline, Michigan.